A Transition Guide for the **"Next Gener**

MW01557848

The Path from Commissions to ***Fee-for-Services***

DANIEL R. MEYLAN

bookVillages

THE PATH FROM COMMISSIONS TO FEE-FOR-SERVICES: A Transition Guide for the "Next Generation" Healthcare Advisor
© 2021 by Daniel R. Meylan

All rights reserved. No part of this publication may be reproduced in any form without written permission from Book Villages, P.O. Box 64526, Colorado Springs, CO 80962. www.bookvillages.com

ISBN: 978-1-94429-887-6

Cover and Interior Design by Scot McDonald

Printed in the United States of America
1 2 3 4 5 6 7 8 9 10 Printing/Year 25 24 23 22 21

Table of Contents

My Fee-for-Services Journey.. 5

Introduction: Old Dogs, New Tricks... 7

Chapter 1: The Need for Transition... 9

Chapter 2: Core Deliverables—The Lifeblood of Fee-for-Services............... 13

Chapter 3: Expertise, Substance, and Value... 21

Chapter 4: The Bones of Business... 25

Chapter 5: Simple, Functional Contracts.. 33

Chapter 6: The Metrics That Matter... 37

Chapter 7: What Am I Worth, Really?... 45

Chapter 8: Transparent, Balanced Compensation................................... 51

Chapter 9: Closing and Locking the Door—Selling Your Fee-for-Services Value Proposition.... 57

Chapter 10: Signatures Matter—Closing the Deal................................... 63

Chapter 11: Systematize Your Operation—No Loose Ends....................... 65

Chapter 12: What's Next?.. 73

Endnotes... 75

My Fee-for-Services Journey

In 1973, almost five decades ago, I was given the opportunity to become a partner in a small property and casualty insurance agency. The bank where I was employed (my first real career position after graduating from college) had a local insurance agency as one of their primary customers. For medical reasons, the owner of that agency approached the owners of the bank about acquiring his business. The next thing I knew, I had launched my insurance career as the producer and manager of a bank-owned insurance agency at the ripe age of twenty-two.

I knew absolutely nothing about insurance, but my partners, who owned the bank, had confidence in my ability to make our agency a success. I quickly learned that insurance had some substantial career and economic benefits that far exceeded the opportunities in my original banking career path. For personal reasons, my time in the agency and with the bank was short, but the confidence my partners had in me was well founded.

Over the ensuing decades, with my teams, we:

- Started four new agencies from scratch
- Developed and managed multiple insurance programs, including self-funded plans and risk retention groups
- Participated in two hundred agency acquisitions and divestitures
- Served as a general agent with underwriting authority
- Acted as the senior agency executive with sales and marketing responsibilities for two hundred P&C and benefits producers generating $100,000,000 in commission income
- Launched a successful private business consulting practice
- Spent eight years as the national sales director of a group health plan third-party administrator

As a senior executive for a national third-party administrator, I was responsible for building the agent distribution network that provided ERISA qualified level-funded and self-funded group health plans.

Fee-for-services arrangements have always been part of my insurance profession. My initial exposure to fee-for-services happened almost by accident. As a commercial insurance agent and agency owner in a rural county seat, I had successfully taken over the commercial insurance package for our county. We substantially upgraded their coverage and reduced costs by delivering a customized public-entity plan offered by one of our carriers.

During that process, I became well acquainted with all the local county commissioners and senior county employees. One of those commissioners referred me to the commissioners in a neighboring county.

That neighboring county had experienced several uncovered claims and wanted someone other than their local agents to review their coverages. I offered to become their agent and place their commercial insurance plan, but they were firm in their position that the county insurance had to be purchased through an agent that resided in the county.

They asked whether I would be willing to work on their behalf under a consulting agreement. That became my first fee-for-services agreement. It turned out well for all parties concerned. Considering this occurred in the early eighties, the fee was generous by any standard. And all parties were satisfied with the outcome. The county had a better insurance plan, the cost was lower, and the local agents retained their county's commercial insurance business.

In the years that followed, the agreement I created with that county became the template for subsequent fee-for-services agreements. Thirty years later, in 2010, I launched a private consulting practice that grew into a thriving business based exclusively on fee-for-services agreements. One of the key aspects of all our fee-for-services agreements is total transparency and disclosure of fees, including the specific services to be offered and how and when fees will be earned and paid.

This workbook (and corresponding workshops) targets insurance agents who live on commission income only and realize that commissions alone may no longer be adequate compensation for their time and expertise. But transitioning to fee-for-services is a process, not an event.

This workbook offers a *Path* to prepare you and your agency to install a fee-for-services business model over several months or years. There will be a period of time when you can expect to use both models. It is likely you may continue to generate a portion of your revenues from commissions. Commission levels are set at the discretion of the carrier and usually do not reflect the full value of the services offered by a Next-Generation Healthcare Advisor.

There are two other critical game changers for the health insurance broker. Today the COVID-19 pandemic has redefined the clinical and financial healthcare landscape in ways no one could have imagined. It will become a matter of business survival for employers to reduce the cost of their health plans. There is now federal law and regulation that requires health insurance brokers to fully disclose direct and indirect compensation on group and individual health plans beginning January 1, 2022.

If you are now being paid by the traditional commission structure, how are you going to get appropriately compensated for delivering those lower-cost health plans? Also, with the strong likelihood that "the public option" or "Medicare for all" will become the primary health insurance option competing against group health plans, commissioned-based employee benefit plans may become extinct. If that happens, the only realistic way to survive and be appropriately compensated is through a fee-for-services agreement with the employer.

This workbook not only provides the necessary fee-for-services concepts and processes but also offers tools to help develop a viable and profitable fee-for-services employee benefits practice.

Introduction: Old Dogs, New Tricks

Every journey includes at least two critical elements. The first element is the destination, which in this case is your own thriving fee-based employee benefits practice. The second element is a map, or a plan that becomes the *Path* to your destination. This workbook and the attendant workshops will become your road map, your *Path*. You will follow the resulting *Path* to your destination. Here are some of the milestones you will see on this journey:

1. Understanding why fee-for-services is even necessary
2. Defining the core deliverables of your fee-for-services business, which are materially different from the core deliverables of a commissioned health insurance brokerage business
3. Learning how to design your fee-for-services value proposition
4. Learning how to build your fee-for-services business model
5. Learning how to build a fee-for-services agreement
6. Learning how to calculate the value of your time
7. Developing key operational performance metrics for you and your practice
8. Learning how to sell your fee-for-services value proposition
9. Learn how and why the fees-for-services model complies with the No Surprises Act requirement that stipulates as of 1-1-2022 all brokers must fully disclose all direct and indirect commission received on individual and group health plans.

I also share concepts on how a fee-for-services practice is affected by technology, errors and omissions insurance, compliance, and the question of perpetuation.

Every journey has its challenges. For most of you who have operated exclusively in a commission-based business structure, the commitment to follow this path will be the hardest part of the journey. Reading through this workbook should help you make that commitment.

Every journey takes time. Part of the process will be determining how quickly you plan to reach the fee-for-services destination. Just like with any journey, you can choose to walk, run, drive, or fly. Regardless of the pace you select, deciding to ignore the concepts in this workbook could prove to be financially fatal.

Welcome to the path from a commission-based insurance business to a thriving fee-for-services employee benefits consulting practice.

Please accept my best wishes for a smooth and successful journey.

CHAPTER 1

The Need for Transition

Delivering group health insurance as an agent or broker has historically been a simple, straightforward, and lucrative profession. It required an insurance license, some product knowledge, the willingness to engage with people, and a modest amount of time. The most appealing part of being a health insurance agent was the lifestyle it provided. The successful agent had the time and resources to live a comfortable, relaxed lifestyle that included a healthy work-life balance. A successful agent built a book of business that delivered a certain level of recurring commission income that supported his or her lifestyle. The bonus was that that recurring revenue had an asset value that was marketable and served as a solid retirement plan.

Then the Affordable Care Act (ACA) happened. Healthcare costs now devour 18 percent of the United States gross domestic product.[1] Since 2010, group health insurance rates have increased twice as fast as wages.[2] Federal and state politicians and regulators have created a dizzying array of insurance and labor laws and regulations, including the recent legislation in the No Surprises Act that requires full disclosure of broker compensation. For the employer, it has become a much greater challenge to operate a thriving business that offers a comprehensive affordable group health plan that complies with all federal and state laws and regulations. Group health insurance carriers, medical providers, and drug

• • •

Since 2010, group health insurance rates have increased twice as fast as wages.

companies collaborated to create systems and processes that maximize their shareholders' earnings at the expense of the healthcare consumer. (Is any one of us not a healthcare consumer?) And it is becoming more likely every day that "the public option" or "Medicare for all" will further disrupt and undermine the role of the group health insurance broker.

The life and career of the group health insurance broker has become much more complex. As healthcare costs continue to rise and compliance complexities increase, a group health insurance plan is no longer a simple sell-

A Next-Generation Healthcare Advisor will be characterized as:

- A trusted strategic partner
- The professional equivalent of the business's attorney or CPA
- A key management team member
- A healthcare risk financing consultant
- A resource for compliance
- A resource for employee education and communications
- A resource for HR leadership and planning support
- An insurance product market access point
- An advocate for the health and well-being of employees and families
- A champion of innovative ways to reduce healthcare costs

and-forget process. Employers are firing their health insurance brokers and hiring qualified Healthcare Advisors who can deliver solutions to the rising cost and increasing complexity of group health plans.

At the same time, group insurance carriers have cut commission income and continue to push more service requirements back on the broker. Insurance carriers are turning to technology to perform many of the functions that the broker and his or her staff performed in the past. The ACA also compressed the group insurance renewal workload into a 120-day window in the fourth quarter of every year. Group health insurance agents now spend twice as many man-hours on any given case as they did ten years ago—at a lower commission level which will now need to be fully disclosed.

The comfortable, relaxed lifestyle of the group health insurance agent has evaporated, replaced by a fast-paced, highly demanding lifestyle with much less time for leisure and family.

Enter the next generation of health insurance professionals. This next generation will not be group health insurance agents; they will be Next-Generation Healthcare Advisors whose primary role will be to manage the healthcare risk of their group clients.

With the fee-for-services approach offered in this workbook, the Healthcare Advisor will be better able to perform these functions while earning an appropriate level of compensation.

Why Shift to a Fee-for-Services Model?

Traditional commission income is no longer adequate to cover the costs and time required to meet the ever-increasing demands of the typical group health insurance client.

Under the current commission model, brokers are working too many hours for free!

Traditional brokers cannot afford to hire competent support staff to help deliver the required services on the commission income they currently receive. They are now required to deliver a scope of services far beyond what was previously expected of health insurance brokers.

Traditional agents are losing money, and their work-life balance is suffering. Given health insurance brokers' potential impact on their clients' bottom line, these traditional brokers are not being appropriately valued.

The typical employer does not fully understand the man-hours, experience, resources, and expertise required to provide a group benefit plan to their company.

Commissions will likely be reduced or eliminated in the future. Since commissions must now be fully disclosed there are those who will strongly suggest that brokers are overpaid and there could be political pressure to reduce or eliminate commissions altogether.

> **Traditional commission income is no longer adequate to cover the costs and time required to meet the ever-increasing demands of the typical group health insurance client.**

If you are a health insurance broker, you need to start the process of becoming a Healthcare Advisor who operates under a fee-for-services agreement. The following chapters of this workbook will support the process of transitioning to a fee-for-services business model.

Deliverables	Status Quo Health Insurance Broker	Healthcare Advisor
Benefit Plan Designs	x	x
Marketplace Options – Carriers, Networks	x	x
Cost Comparisons	x	x
Commissions	x	
Compliance HIPAA, ERISA, DOLX		x
Self-Funding & Level-Funding Structure		x
Medical Underwriting		x
Education–Employer & Employees		x
Regulatory Reporting		x
Claims Analysis & Review		x
Plan Integrations–TPA, PDM, UCR		
Reference-Based Pricing		x
Direct Primary Care		x
Long Term Strategic Planning		x
Performance-Based Fees-for-Service		x
Time	40 Hours per Account/Year	70 Hours per Account/Year

The Path from Commissions to *Fee-for-Services*

Why Fee-for-Services Makes Sense

Fee-for-services is about value, time, and money. Assume you have a twenty-life group that generates $7,000 in annual commissions. As the health insurance agent, you spend forty man-hours in the course of the year preparing the renewal, shopping various markets, designing a benefit structure, delivering the proposal, facilitating enrollment meetings, supporting employees who have claims issues, adding and deleting employees, communicating with the business owner, and dealing with the carrier on service and billing issues.

You are earning $175 per hour. Now increase the required man-hours from forty to sixty hours because you are moving your client to a level-funded plan that is medically underwritten. You now have various state and federal compliance issues that must be addressed with the business owner. The level-funded carrier also provides detailed claims reports, which need to be reviewed with the business owner. Additionally, you must spend time educating the employer and employees about managing the cost of healthcare within the plan and supporting your client as they grow and add new staff.

If the commission income on that case remains at $7,000, your earnings just dropped by 33 percent to $117 per hour. You just took a 33 percent cut in income. You are doing more work for less compensation.

Remember your commission income or hourly billing rate not only pays your personal income but also covers all the operating expenses of your agency—including staff salaries, occupancy charges, marketing and sales expenses, technology costs, education and training, administrative costs, and income taxes.

More work for less money is not a sustainable business strategy, completely aside from the implications on your work-life balance.

> **Your commission income or hourly billing rate not only pays your personal income but also covers all the operating expenses.**

CHAPTER 2

Core Deliverables—The Lifeblood of Fee-for-Services

The core deliverable of the group health insurance agent is a group health insurance policy.

That is not the core deliverable of the Healthcare Advisor.

The core deliverable of the Next-Generation Healthcare Advisor is heathcare risk finance and management.

What is a core deliverable? The core deliverable of Ford Motor Company, General Motors, Honda, Mazda, Mercedes-Benz, Chrysler, and Subaru is transportation. The

> **The core deliverable of the Next-Generation Healthcare Advisor is healthcare risk management.**

core deliverable is unique for every business but always starts with a single common denominator like transportation. Where that

Your Core Deliverable

Unique for every business ...

Your core deliverable is _____.

- Specific Skill, Product, or Service
- **Value Proposition**
- **Differentiation**
- Quality Competence
- Technical Knowledge
- Industry Knowledge and Language
- Distribution, Vendors, Suppliers

The Path from Commissions to *Fee-for-Services*

core deliverable becomes unique is how it is packaged for the customer.

There are several variables to consider when developing any core-deliverable strategy. So let's unpack each of these to get a clearer picture of how a Next-Generation Healthcare Advisor might build his or her new core deliverable of healthcare risk management.

Your Specific Skill, Product, or Service

The Healthcare Advisor is not just selling a group health insurance policy or plan. Delivering healthcare risk management implies the following:

- A broader scope of work
- A higher level of technical skill
- A different process and a different outcome from selling policies

- Delivering peace of mind and lower financial risk
- Ongoing engagement as opposed to just making a sale
- A higher value for the services rendered

However, that higher value must be communicated and justified.

What are the components of your core deliverable, healthcare risk management?

- Your specific skill, product, or service
- Your value proposition
- Your market differentiation
- Your level of competence
- Your technical knowledge
- Your knowledge of the industry and industry language
- Your relationships with vendors and suppliers

Your Value Proposition

What is a value proposition? Think about it in these terms: Mercedes-Benz and BMW have different value propositions from Kia and Subaru. There are distinct differences in the product design, quality, and cost; the target market; and the look and message of their marketing. The companies have the same core deliverable, but they serve distinctly different markets with a distinctly different transportation solution. So what is your unique value proposition as a Healthcare Advisor? Are you a Mercedes-Benz or a Subaru?

Why is it so important that you have a clearly defined value proposition targeted at a specific type of employer? Employers are just as unique as individuals, with each employer group defined by their leadership and culture, their products, and their marketplace. Employers expect their group health plan to not only serve their employees but also integrate with their leadership style and

Value Proposition

> What is it?
> How do we find it?
> Is it unique?
> Does it differentiate our business in the marketplace?

> **Employers are just as unique as individuals, with each employer group defined by their leadership and culture, their products, and their marketplace.**

business culture. Different employers have different expectations about their group health plans. Some expectations are unrealistic: a Mercedes expectation on a Prius budget would be a guaranteed failure in the fee-for-services world. But if that employer has a Mercedes expectation, recognizes the value of that expectation, and is ready to write the check—that becomes a win for everyone. That does not mean the employer with the Prius mindset will not become a solid client, but you as the Healthcare Advisor need to tailor your value proposition and operational cost structure to an economy mindset.

The first question to consider is, *Who is the market you are going to serve?* The most successful and prominent Healthcare Advisors are focused on a vertical market. You need to determine yours. Who are you going to serve? Anybody or everybody is the wrong answer. Select a market segment you want to serve—presumably one that corresponds to your passion, knowledge, and expertise. This will become vitally important later in this workbook as you build your business model.

Obviously, a value proposition is defined by the price you charge and the quality and technical capability you offer the client. Ultimately, with a fee-for-services business model, you are going to contract your clients at a billable hourly rate as opposed to collecting a commission. You may convert that billable hourly rate or offer a performance-based fee agreement to a per employee, per month (PEPM) fee, but that fee still needs to reflect your cost of doing business.

Mercedes-Benz and Cadillac serve the luxury market and deliver highly crafted, technologically advanced, quiet, comfortable, and expensive vehicles. The Toyota Prius and Chevy Volt offer incredible efficiency in small, modestly priced, technologically advanced vehicles. Ford and Chevrolet offer low-cost to luxury pickup trucks designed to be utilitarian while at the same time comfortable, easy to drive, and full of technological advances. Each product serves a different market and has a unique cost and value proposition.

As a Healthcare Advisor, what are you going to be?

- Prius or Volt: serving the small-employer market efficiently at a modest cost
- A Ford pickup truck: serving a market that needs utility and comfort with prices ranging from low cost to luxury
- A Mercedes: serving the luxury market with state-of-the-art technology and maximum comfort at a luxury price

This workbook is devoted to helping you develop your value proposition. These questions address the basic components of your unique value proposition:

- Who are my core customers?
- What are their needs?
- What is our contracted hourly rate?
- How do we justify that contracted hourly rate?
- Are my fees totally transparent?

Market Differentiation

The next key question is, *How do we differentiate ourselves from the competition in the mind of our customer?* This is a branding, marketing, and behavior question. The average group health insurance agent is viewed as a peddler who sells a policy, collects a commission, and offers no real solutions to the rising cost of group healthcare plans. The purpose of the Healthcare Advisor is to offer creative and effective solutions to healthcare costs. The better question is, *How can you communicate your unique Healthcare Advisor purpose in order to differentiate yourself from the traditional group health insurance agent?* And then taking this idea one additional step, *How does your firm differentiate itself from the firms of other Healthcare Advisors?*

If you are shifting from being a group health insurance agent to being a Healthcare Advisor, the process will not be easy, especially if you already have a block of clients who see you as their agent.

Six material shifts need to take place to move from a health insurance agent to a Healthcare Advisor. The shifts need to happen in this order over time:

- A shift in belief. *I believe I need to become an advisor!*
- A shift in thinking. *I need to completely rethink my approach to serving my clients!*
- A shift in behavior. *I will stop behaving like an agent and start behaving like an advisor!*
- A shift in processes. *I will rebuild my business processes to deliver solutions for a fee, not policies for a commission!*
- A shift in outcomes. *I will accept all the changes required to make the transition to an advisor!*
- A shift to compensation transparency. *I will be completely transparent about my fee structure!*

Differentiation in the marketplace takes time, courage, commitment, and hard work. But the most difficult part of the process is making and keeping the commitment to change your own beliefs and behaviors. This workbook will offer tools to make that road easier to travel.

Competence

Establishing yourself as a Healthcare Advisor requires high levels of competence in multiple technical, strategic, and leadership skills. For the most part, group health insurance brokers are salespeople. They are viewed that way by the employers and employees they serve. In contrast, Healthcare Advisors are leaders. Leaders drive change. Leaders cannot become and remain leaders without competence, and they must have a broad set of competencies:

- Big-picture thinking
- Listening with humility
- Constant learning and personal improvement
- Identifying and removing obstacles
- Learning from the past to adapt to the future
- Communicating, training, and educating
- Saying no with confidence
- Delivering quality outcomes
- Growing people and building teams
- Utilizing performance metrics

Technical Knowledge

When an agent sells a group insurance plan, he or she focuses on the technical aspects of the insurance policy—those policy terms, the policy service, the policy claims administration, the billings, and regulatory compliance. All are responsibilities delegated to others, typically insurance carrier employees, their representatives, or the technology platforms deployed by the insurance company.

As a Healthcare Advisor, you accept the responsibility of designing and managing the entire life cycle of an employer's group health plan. Accepting and delivering on that commitment will require a high level of technical competence for every phase of that life cycle. The Healthcare Advisor will need to be competent in the following technical disciplines:

1. Healthcare risk financing, structure, and variables
2. Evaluation of the client's healthcare risk profile
3. Review of the historical healthcare risk costs
4. Third-party administrator business models
5. Stop-loss insurance carrier underwriting appetites
6. Medical underwriting methodologies
7. Customized benefit plans that match the client's culture and business objectives
8. Tools and strategies to control healthcare-cost drivers—direct primary care, transparent vendors, and aggressive claims strategies
9. Healthcare provider negotiations
10. Alternative cost reimbursement methodologies—narrow networks, PPO, HMO, reference-based pricing, bundled pricing, and negotiated contracts
11. Employer education
12. Employee enrollment, education, and engagement
13. Technology tools for enrollment, management, and service
14. A working knowledge of the rate and cost impact of chronic and critical illnesses
15. Federal and state healthcare laws and regulations—ERISA, HIPAA, and COBRA
16. Federal and state labor laws and regulations
17. Pending and proposed federal and state laws and regulations
18. Tax-advantaged plans—FSA, HSA, and HRA
19. Ancillary products—dental, vision, LTD, STD, voluntary, and gap plans
20. Compliance reporting—DOL, IRS, and HHS
21. Ongoing claims cost analysis and review
22. Understanding of the client's business objectives
23. Understanding of the client's industry
24. Regular strategic planning sessions with the employer's key leadership

In the arena of healthcare financing and healthcare consumption, the "Return on Investment" for deliberate, focused education will always be significant.

One firm (notice I did not call them an agency) that has been incredibly successful has built their entire fee-for-services value proposition around their ability to educate clients and potential clients. They are highly competent in every technical area listed above, but their primary focus is education.

Every member of the firm is trained to be an educator. They are laser focused on creating informed business owners, business leaders, employees, healthcare consumers, and healthcare providers. Everything they do starts with education. Careful, intentional education takes time and money. They reject any potential client who is not committed to the investment in time and money required to educate company leadership, employees, and other plan members.

In the arena of healthcare financing and healthcare consumption, the ROI for deliberate, focused education will always be significant. Education is this firm's primary technical skill and key market differentiator. Not only is their business—all based on fee-for-services—highly profitable, but all employees are well compensated, have an ownership interest in the company, and share in the profits. This firm

• • •

Healthcare spending consumes nearly 20 percent of this country's gross domestic product.

uses education to build trust with clients and demonstrate that they maximize the return on the investment the employer is making in their employees.

Knowledge of the Industry and Industry Language

As mentioned earlier, healthcare spending consumes nearly 20 percent of this country's gross domestic product.[3] It is also one of the primary drivers of the growing federal budget deficit. Healthcare is a vast, complex industry where billions of dollars are exchanged every day. The Healthcare Advisor must be an avid student of all aspects of this industry. Keeping up with and truly understanding it is a massive undertaking and requires constant study and analysis. As this industry evolves, it will be the responsibility of the Healthcare Advisor to interpret for clients how those changes will affect the cost and delivery of group health plans. A key component of the Healthcare Advisor's value proposition is the ability to navigate the healthcare industry on behalf of clients in such a way that long-term costs are reduced, employees are satisfied, and company business objectives are achieved.

The Healthcare Advisor must be able to simplify and synthesize all this information into terms their client can understand, then communicate exactly how all these factors will affect that client's business future.

Every industry has its own language. The inability to communicate effectively will always marginalize the core deliverable of any enterprise. Unfortunately for the consumer, there are multiple languages (different types of industry "speak") present in the healthcare market. The Healthcare Advisor needs to be fluent in all of them:

1. Healthcare speak
2. Medication speak
3. Insurance speak
4. Network speak
5. Risk financing speak
6. Medical underwriting speak
7. Compliance speak
8. Technology speak
9. Business speak
10. Your client's industry speak
11. Consumer speak
12. Regulatory speak
13. Political speak
14. Media speak

There are several more languages that are not included in this list. All these "speaks" add to the complexity and confusion present in the healthcare industry. But complexity and confusion create opportunity. Truly brilliant Healthcare Advisors become translators of all these languages for their clients and plan members. To translate is to explain a concept simply in a way that enables the listener to answer the question, *What does this terminology mean for me today and in the future?* Any Healthcare Advisor who is competent in all these languages and has the ability to translate them effectively can justify executive-level compensation.

Relationships with Vendors and Suppliers

Since every self-funded or level-funded group health plan involves multiple vendors and suppliers of products and services, the Healthcare Advisor becomes the quarterback of a team. That team is made up of vendors who block and tackle, suppliers who specialize in defense or offense, water boys on the sidelines, referees on the field, and fans in the stands. They are all part of the game, but the quarterback always gets the ball. The quarterback receives coaching and game plans from the sidelines, but he or she is responsible for the execution. Nobody wins the game or makes it to the playoffs without a competent quarterback.

A successful Healthcare Advisor drives a team of highly qualified, competent vendors and suppliers who are an integral part of their healthcare advisory team. Some vendors are superstars in their own right and help get the team, the fans, and the quarterback to the playoffs. But some vendors are marginal and drop the ball or fail to execute the plays. The quarterback, the Healthcare Advisor, must have a vital relationship with and understanding of all the players on the team. *Who are they? What do they bring to the field? How do they fit in the playbook? What will I expect of them when a play is called?*

Therefore, the Healthcare Advisor needs to assemble a team of suppliers and vendors and understand their deliverables, strengths, and weaknesses, as well as their ability to execute under pressure. As you are selecting vendors and suppliers, one of the key elements to look for will be a commitment to total transparency about all fees.

The health insurance industry is notorious for putting hidden fees inside group health plans without full disclosure to the plan sponsors. With the pending requirement to disclose all direct and indirect compensation to the plan sponsor, those "hidden" fees will now become very transparent and will require the broker to justify why they are entitled to those "fees." Successful Healthcare Advisory Firms operating on a fee-for-services basis will be built around solid working relationships with competent, motivated, responsive, transparent vendors and suppliers.

Notes

CHAPTER 3

Expertise, Substance, and Value

We need to dig a little deeper into how you, as a *Healthcare Advisor*, build your own value proposition. This is much more than a branding exercise; it is the discovery of whom you want to be and how you are going to deliver yourself and your firm to your prospects and clients. If you are seriously considering transitioning from commissions to fee-for-services, you will have to spend time formulating a value proposition that works for you.

What Is Your Value Proposition?

Here is a list of key topics and related questions you will need to answer honestly to start building your unique value proposition as a *Healthcare Advisor*. You may want to engage your trusted peers and advisors, both personal and professional, in this process.

PERSONAL INVENTORY
1. What is my behavior style?
2. What are my personal strengths and weaknesses?
3. What are my professional strengths and weaknesses?
4. What are my financial resources?
5. What is my driving motivation?
6. What do I hope to achieve?
   a. For my family?
   b. For my peers and employees?
   c. For my clients?
   d. For my industry?
   e. For my community?

VISION OF THE FUTURE
1. What does the perfect long-term outcome look like?

MANAGEMENT OF CHANGE
1. How will I transition?
2. What needs to end?
3. What needs to begin?
4. Am I willing to work under a contract?
5. Am I willing to be totally transparent about my fees?

MARKET REALITIES
1. What is my ideal market?
2. What does my ideal market need?
3. What is the economic reality of my ideal market?
4. Whom do I not want to serve?
5. Who is the competition in my ideal market?
6. What is the future of my ideal market?

7. What are the unknowns and potential risks?
8. What are the potential rewards?

TIMELINE
1. When do I start?
2. How long will this take?

METRICS
1. What do I need to learn about critical metrics?
2. Where do I find support resources to establish benchmarks?
3. How do I evaluate the performance of vendors, partners, and staff?
4. What is my value per hour today?
5. What does my value per hour need to be?
6. How do I grow my value per hour?
7. Do I have the courage and commitment to execute this transition?

I am sure these questions will lead you to many more questions. The following chapters will help you sort out your answers. To continue the vehicle metaphor, you need to decide whether you are a Prius, a Subaru, a Ford pickup, or a Mercedes. If you do this work and honestly respond to these questions, your value proposition should become clear.

Can You Justify Your Value Proposition?

Let's assume, after going through your planning process and answering all the questions listed above, you determine that the value of your time is $250 per hour. How will you justify that value? The answer is simple: your client must see and believe that you bring more than $250 per hour of value. The skills and services you deliver must make a measurable economic difference to all the stakeholders affected by your deliverables.

> **Differentiation is not as difficult as it sounds, but it is vitally important. As Healthcare Advisors it is vital that we become distinct from the commissioned health insurance agent.**

As we get further into this workbook, we will provide the tools and processes to enable you to justify your value as a Healthcare Advisor at the hourly value you set for yourself.

Can You Clearly Communicate Your Value Proposition?

After you have set your value at $250, $350, or $450 per hour, how will you communicate that value to your prospect or client? We will devote an entire chapter to that topic.

How Are You Differentiating Yourself and Your Organization with Your Value Proposition?

Differentiation is not as difficult as it sounds, but it is vitally important. As Healthcare Advisors it is vital that we become distinct from the commissioned health insurance agent. But beyond that, as you build your value proposition, you must carefully craft your message, select your target market, build your processes, and design your deliverables to separate your fee-for-services Healthcare Advisor practice from other Healthcare Advisors. How might this look?

1. You select a narrow target market such as HVAC contractors, government

contractors, auto dealers, nonprofits, women-owned businesses, or farm co-ops—and become a recognized expert in dealing with the unique business requirements within their group health plans.
2. You build world-class expertise in certain disciplines and processes such as employee communication and education, medical underwriting, medication management, claims analysis, ERISA compliance, healthcare risk financing, healthcare risk management, provider negotiations, direct primary care, or reference-based pricing—to name a few possibilities.

Your differentiation must be unique and identifiable by your clients and their members/employees.

Are You Prepared to Stand Behind Your Value Proposition?

As you build out your value proposition as a fee-for-services Healthcare Advisor, keep in mind you will need to defend that value proposition. These are the two keys to effectively defending your value proposition:

1. Remain focused on and committed to the market you have chosen to serve.
2. Create and communicate a set of key performance metrics that demonstrate the value you bring to your group clients and the industry.

Toyota is able to stand behind the Prius because the car has a proprietary technology that delivers incredible fuel efficiency. Mercedes-Benz is able to stand behind their S-Class because it delivers the ultimate luxury driving experience.

Notes

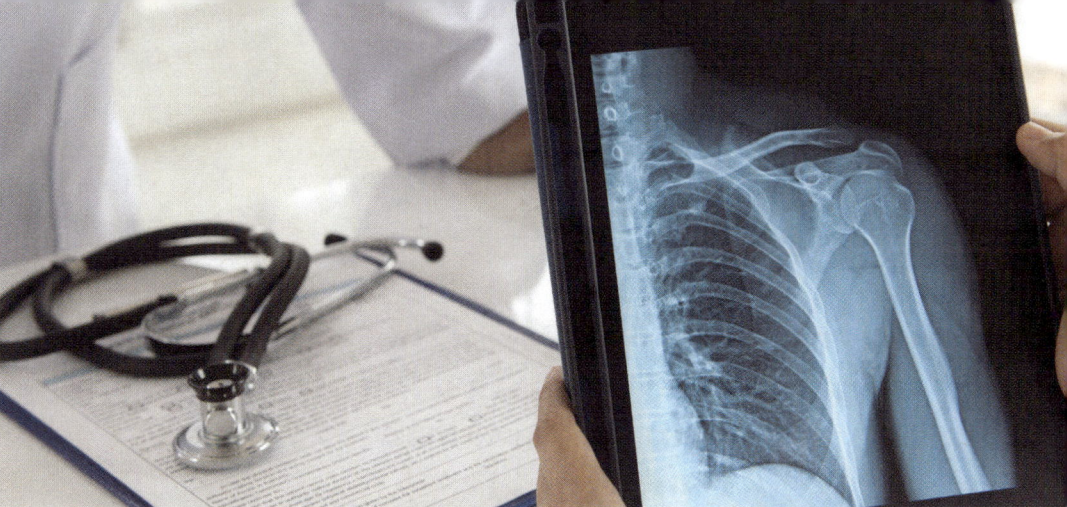

CHAPTER 4

The Bones of Business

Building a new business model and business plan requires effort, patience, thought, focus, and discipline. No two models or plans are the same, but they all have common characteristics and required components. Missing or ignoring one or more of those key components will render the business model ineffective at best and fatally flawed at worst.

The core deliverable and value proposition discussed in the prior chapters are the centerpiece of every business model. But around the core deliverable are eight competencies required in every business.

Those eight elements are *planning*, *sales*, *marketing*, *leadership*, *finance*, *administration*, *human resources*, and *systems*.

Each of these elements has equal value. How they are interconnected will be unique to your business model. You will be highly competent at some of these elements and marginally competent at others. Since we are building an entirely new fee-for-services business model, we will focus on two of the primary elements in this chart: *planning* and *leadership*.

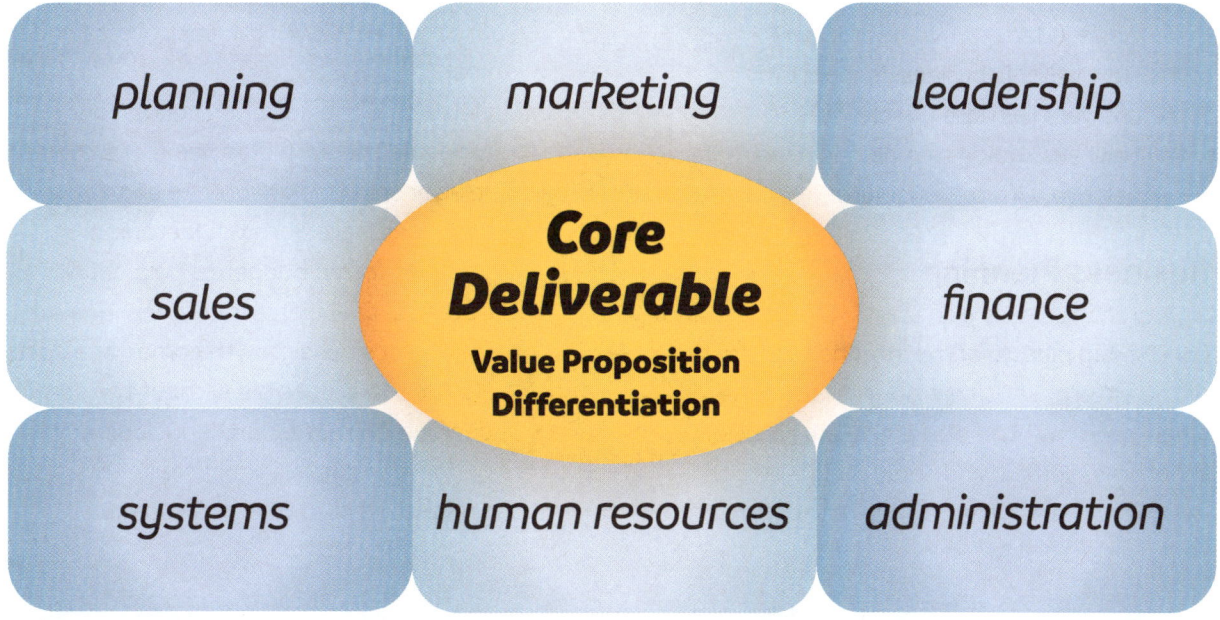

The Path from Commissions to *Fee-for-Services*

Planning

> *"If you have a business plan before you have a life plan, your business will become your life."*
> —Daniel Meylan

Life Planning

The business planning discussion should always start with your life plan. Your business should be a vehicle to carry you and your loved ones to your (collective) personal goals. We have all seen people who made a business their top priority and destroyed their families, their health, and their reputation.

So here are some key life-planning questions:

1. For whom am I responsible, besides myself?
2. What are my responsibilities to those I love?
3. What do I want for the future of those I love?
4. What are my life priorities?
5. What legacy do I want to leave?
6. How will this business support my answers to these questions?
7. How am I going to maintain a work-life balance with this business?

Business Planning

A great business plan starts with a clear and concise big picture of the intended destination of the enterprise. Where do we want to be, by when, and why? The plan articulates a vision that is measurable and compelling. Once the destination is set, the balance of the plan is devoted to answering the who, what, where, when, and why questions around each of the other core business competencies. A business plan becomes an action road map with specific tasks, deadlines, processes, and assignments. Most business plans that fail focus on just finances and not the core business elements that drive the finances.

Budgeting

A budget is a financial road map to building a business. If you are transitioning from a commission model to a fee-for-services model, a budget is absolutely essential. A budget is about cash flow, timing, income, expenses, and profits. If you are currently operating a thriving, profitable, commissioned-based business, you have a solid foundation on which to build a fee-for-services operating budget. You know your current cash flow, income, expenses, and profitability. You can modify your existing budget to model how your fee-based income can be integrated over time and eventually replace your commission income. Here are the suggested steps to building a fee-for-services budget:

1. Create a pro forma budget based on the income, expenses, and operating profit of your business over the past two calendar years.
2. Determine the current value of your time and the projected value of a client relationship (see chapters 6 and 7).
3. Apply estimated growth factors to your pro forma budget to help define potential financial results. Keep in mind that all business growth comes at a cost. No growth is possible without the careful deployment of resources, including human capital, relational capital, financial capital, and chronological capital.

Distribution Planning

Distribution planning involves coordinating and integrating all the elements of your core deliverable for the benefit of your employer clients and their employees. Who provides what services to the employer? When, how, and at what cost, and how are those services paid for?

One or two people attempting to deliver every aspect of a group-healthcare risk-financing plan is a flawed strategy. Vendors and suppliers will become a vital part of your core deliverable. They must be evaluated based on their competence, capacity, cost, and relevance to the needs of the client. You, as the Healthcare Advisor, must coordinate the collective activities of these distributors for the benefit of the client. Delivering cost-effective, appropriately designed, and efficiently delivered group health plans is a team sport, and the Healthcare Advisor is the quarterback who will only be as good as his team!

Contingency Planning

This is known as what-if planning. Most organizations fail miserably at this exercise. Given the volatile nature of healthcare and the dollars involved, it is a forgone conclusion that there will be dramatic changes in availability, cost, and quality of healthcare over the next ten to twenty years. Change is inevitable (hello, COVID-19).

These are the types of questions that should be asked. What happens to a fee-for-services business:

- Since all revenues earned on a case must now be disclosed prior to the sale?
- If "The public option" or "Medicare for all" becomes a reality?
- If commissions are eliminated entirely?
- If employer-paid group benefits become subject to income tax at federal and state levels?
- If the number of available physicians continues to decline?
- If healthcare costs become unaffordable?
- If employers stop offering healthcare plans?
- If federal insurance regulation preempts all state insurance regulation?
- If personal income tax rates triple?
- If we have a worldwide economic recession?

Here are the key questions to ask when considering the possibilities above:

1. How would this affect our practice?
2. How would we adapt to the new reality?
3. How would we need to adapt our core deliverable and value proposition?

Perpetuation Planning

Does a fee-for-services Next-Generation Healthcare Advisory Firm have the same market value as a traditional employee benefits agency? Can a fee-for-services Healthcare Advisory Firm be considered a marketable asset that could be sold to a third party? The answer is yes—subject to certain conditions. A fee-for-services Healthcare Advisory Firm built around an individual who must always be active and present has little, if any, market value. A fee-for-services Healthcare Advisory Firm that employs competent professionals and has a consistent history of revenue growth and profitability will always have a solid market value.

Leadership

Great leadership is the primary catalyst of change. Changing to a fee-for-services business model will require great leadership.

Leadership

- **Big-Picture Focus**
- **Discipline and Creative Thinking**
- **Planning and Decision-Making**
- **Risk Management**
- **Deployment of Resources**
- **Performance Measurement**
- **Accountability**
- **Delegation and Motivation**

The purpose of this workbook is to provide the leader guidance in transitioning from a commission-based employee benefits practice to a fee-for-services Healthcare Advisory Firm.

Big-Picture Focus

Great leadership starts with big-picture focus, which requires the leader to:

1. Paint a vision of the big picture for his or her new fee-for-services practice;
2. Make certain all actions, processes, and initiatives serve the big picture;
3. Eliminate all distractions from achieving the big picture;
4. Modify the big picture as outside forces affect the original big-picture vision.

Discipline and Creative Thinking

Great leaders are disciplined and creative. The primary characteristic of a disciplined leader is the ability to use time well and follow a structured process. The mature leader uses a structured approach to evaluate his or her thoughts and communication.

My own critical-thinking style is to see problems as opportunities. I draw visual representations of problems so I can begin to see all the elements of the problem and formulate solutions that can be easily communicated.

> *Immature leaders believe they have all the answers. Mature leaders know they don't and are always challenging themselves to make sure they understand all the variables in the problem they are trying to solve.*

Creative thinking means looking at issues from all angles and seeing what others don't. No two people have the same perspective on any problem or opportunity. Great leaders always use creative thinking to see the problem they face from perspectives other than their own. As you begin the journey of transitioning to a fee-for-services practice, you need to look at your concepts and plans through multiple lenses. You need to become a thought leader. Immature leaders believe they have all the answers. Mature leaders know they don't and are always challenging themselves to make sure they understand all the variables in the problem they are trying to solve.

Planning and Decision-Making

We unpacked the topic of planning in some detail already. But planning without the courage to execute the plan makes the planning process an exercise in futility. The decision to change your practice from commissions to fee-for-services, by its very nature, is a tough decision. You can build the best possible fee-for-services transition plan, but until you execute that decision, the plan is worthless. There comes the day when you finally decide, "Let's do it." Unfortunately, that one decision requires you to make many more decisions. The purpose of solid planning is to prepare a process by which the follow-up decisions are made. You will have to make these kinds of tough decisions:

1. How are we going to communicate our new fee-for-services business model to existing clients?
2. How do we transition our current clients to fee-for-services?
3. Will we be able to maintain all our current clients?
4. Are we willing to give up clients who are not willing to transition to our fee-for-services model?

All these questions are much easier to answer if you have a solid plan. The real question is, *Do you have the courage and the discipline to make the hard decisions to execute your plan?*

Risk Management

The essence of business is taking risk. Those who manage business risk well thrive. Those who do not identify and deal appropriately with business risk will struggle and fail. Transitioning from commissions to fee-for-services comes with substantial risk. The purpose of a solid business plan is to reduce your risk to manageable levels. The good news about risk is this: *the bigger the risk, the bigger the potential reward.* Transitioning to a fee-for-services practice will have multiple rewards, provided the risks involved are well managed. Those rewards may include the following:

1. Better compensation
2. Better quality of life
3. Better client relations
4. Better business stability and long-term growth

Deployment of Resources

Solid leaders who execute dynamic business plans effectively manage every resource at their disposal. Poor leaders fail to correctly identify and deploy all their resources. The leader's task is to deploy resources in such a way as to maximize the performance of the business. A leader has access to many more resources than just money and time. I like to use the word *capital* when talking about resources. Here are the key types of capital to consider when transitioning from

> The long-term success of your fee-for-services practice will hinge on your leadership and your reliance on accurate performance indicators.

a commission-based practice to a fee-for-services model.

Chronological Capital	time
Intellectual Capital	creativity, capacity to solve problems
Relational Capital	depth of relationship, trust
Human Capital	skilled work
Financial Capital	cash, income, earnings, savings, equity
Systemic Capital	technology, systems, processes
Opportunity Capital	first impressions, new markets, new relationships
Emotional Capital	joy, satisfaction
Cultural Capital	environment, team synergy, collaboration
Community Capital	industry, city, state, nation

Performance Measurement

Great leaders are always measuring performance throughout their organizations. A captain pilots the ship or airplane and watches the dials. The long-term success of your fee-for-services practice will hinge on your leadership and your reliance on accurate performance indicators.

In a future chapter, we will dig into the topic of metrics and key performance indicators (KPIs) in more detail. Metrics are tools that help the leader drive the business forward. Visualize a dashboard on a car or an airplane with dials and screens that monitor critical functions. Every business should have a "dashboard" that shows the health and progress of the business. Obviously, one of the most important dials on the dashboard shows profitability. However, there is much more to performance measurement than just how much revenue is generated. Profitability is always a function of people, processes, agreements, and activities that need to be monitored.

In a commission-driven insurance practice, profitability is dependent on a contractual relationship between the agency and the carrier who issues the commission checks. The agency has zero control over the performance or activities of the carrier, but the agency's financial results are ultimately dependent on the performance of the carrier.

In a fee-for-services model, profitability is

a function of a direct contractual relationship between your practice and the client. Those agreements can be adjusted according to the demands of the client and the scope of services you are providing.

Accountability

Under a commission-based compensation structure, true accountability for your skill and services is somewhat obscure. As an agent, you are held accountable only for delivering a policy. Other services you choose to deliver do not affect your income. However, when you transition to a fee-for-services practice and provide your client with a detailed scope of services, the employer now has a basis for holding you accountable for the timely and effective delivery of those services. If you are not prepared to maintain that level of accountability, you are not a good candidate for a fee-for-services practice.

Once you shift to a fee-for-services agreement, your business becomes much more transparent, and you become much more accountable for your actions and the actions of your staff, vendors, and suppliers. But the toughest person to hold accountable is always the one in the mirror.

As a leader, you set the ethical and performance standards for yourself and others. If you fail to hold yourself to your own standards, you will find it virtually impossible to hold others to any standard. Great leaders set high standards and hold themselves accountable first and then have systems and processes in place to hold their teams to those standards.

Delegation and Motivation

In a dynamic fee-for-services practice, you will be continually building client teams that include yourself, your staff, your vendors and suppliers, the client's leaders, the client's employees, and medical providers. Each case will have its own unique team. You will have to assemble that team, prepare them for the game, and coach them through it. Great leaders are gifted at delegating responsibility and motivating all the team members to create a smooth-functioning unit. The real challenge in moving from a commission-based model to a fee-based model is motivating everyone involved, including yourself, to embrace the change. That will be a challenge—but if you are successful, everybody wins!

Notes

CHAPTER 5

Simple, Functional Contracts

A vital element of the fee-for-services model is the fee-for-services agreement. This agreement is a binding legal contract between the advisor's firm and the client/employer. The agreement specifies the terms and conditions for both parties and clearly defines the scope of services to be provided by you and your firm. In this chapter we will examine a sample fee-for-services agreement.

This is only a sample, and I strongly suggest that you craft your own basic agreement. I also strongly recommend that you engage a competent attorney to review your agreement—the ideal lawyer is one who is familiar with both insurance language and the vertical market in which you intend to practice. Once you have a basic fee-for-services agreement that has been reviewed by your legal counsel, it can become your standard operating document.

These are the key elements of any fee-for-services agreement:

1. The legal names and address of the parties to the agreement
2. The effective date of the agreement
3. The general purpose of the agreement
4. A detailed presentation of the scope of services to be offered
5. The terms of the agreement
6. Renewal and termination provisions
7. Provisions of authority and responsibility
8. Terms of payment
9. An indemnification clause
10. Successor and transfer clauses
11. A jurisdictional clause

Scope of Services

The heart of your fee-for-services agreement will be the scope of services statement. This statement summarizes the deliverables that justify your value proposition and your fee structure. We suggest you start building your own scope of services by creating a list of all the services you intend to provide.

The following sample agreement has a possible scope of services statement. It is not all inclusive or intended as a scope of services that you should embrace.

Healthcare Risk Advisor Services SAMPLE AGREEMENT

(Name of Client)

Healthcare Risk Advisor Services Agreement

(This agreement is an illustration only. As a Healthcare Advisor, you should have your legal counsel assist with crafting your fee-for-services agreement.)

Date: Date agreement is offered
To: Name and title of primary contact person (signatory on this agreement)
        Name of business entity
CC: Secondary contacts and involved persons

From: Name of person delivering services
        Name of firm

Re: Healthcare Risk Management Services

Agreement

This document shall serve as an agreement for professional healthcare risk management services provided by (name and address of Healthcare Advisor), hereinafter known as "Advisor," to (name and address of employer, primary owner, or primary decision-maker), hereinafter referred to as "Client/Employer."

The services provided to Client/Employer shall include a review and analysis of the healthcare risks and the preparation and delivery of a comprehensive healthcare risk financing plan, per the scope of services outlined in this agreement. This agreement may be extended to include other activities as mutually agreed. The Advisor's services shall be that of a consultant offering professional services to the Client/Employer as summarized and agreed to in the scope of services listed below.

This document shall serve as the agreement for the terms and conditions of work to be performed, roles and responsibilities, and fees to be paid.

The Advisor shall provide to the Client/Employer those specific services listed and initialed as follows:

____ Understand and support the Client/Employer's business objectives.
____ Develop expertise about unique aspects of the Client/Employer's industry.
____ Conduct periodic strategic planning with the Client/Employer's key leadership.
____ Conduct ongoing claims cost analysis and communicate results to the Client/Employer.
____ Support the Client/Employer in adapting to changing regulatory and political actions.
____ Provide the Client/Employer with cost-effective healthcare risk financing options.
____ Evaluate the structure and variables of the Client/Employer's current healthcare risk financing plan.
____ Evaluate the Client/Employer's healthcare risk profile.

Healthcare Risk Advisor Services SAMPLE AGREEMENT

____ Prepare and deliver a periodic review of the Client/Employer's healthcare claims activity.

____ Review the Client/Employer's historical healthcare plan costs (healthcare risk audit).

____ Evaluate and recommend the services of a third-party administrator or fully insured carrier.

____ Evaluate and recommend stop-loss insurance solutions.

____ Prepare all medical underwriting data to enable appropriate healthcare risk financing solutions.

____ Customize benefit-plan designs that match the Client/Employer's culture and business objectives.

____ Provide tools and strategies to control the Client/Employer's healthcare costs.

____ Evaluate and recommend cost-reduction alternatives including but not limited to direct primary care, reference-based pricing, and transparent vendors.

____ Engage in healthcare provider negotiations on behalf of the Client/Employer, and when appropriate, offer plan member support for the resolution of claims.

____ Evaluate and recommend alternative cost-reimbursement methodologies including but not limited to narrow networks, PPO, HMO, reference-based pricing, bundled pricing, negotiated contracts, and transparent PBMs.

____ Provide ongoing Client/Employer education on current events and issues related to group-healthcare risk financing and compliance.

____ Hold employee enrollment meetings.

____ Provide periodic employee education on healthcare consumption.

____ Provide systems and technology to support proactive employee engagement and plan administration.

____ Evaluate and communicate to the Client/Employer the cost impact of chronic and critical illnesses in the group.

____ Support compliance with relevant federal and state healthcare laws and regulations such as ERISA, HIPAA, and COBRA.

____ Support compliance with relevant federal and state labor laws and regulations.

____ Communicate the possible impact of pending or proposed federal and state policy changes.

____ Prepare and present appropriate tax-advantaged plans such as FSA, HSA, and HRA.

____ Prepare and present appropriate ancillary products including but not limited to dental, vision, LTD, STD, voluntary, and gap plans.

Terms and Conditions:
1. The Advisor shall have no authority to handle cash or commit the Client/Employer and any affiliated entities to any financial obligation, legal contract, insurance contract, or similar obligation without written approval of the Client/Employer.
2. The Client/Employer shall make available to the Advisor any and all technical, financial, operational, and insurance carrier data required to fulfill the obligations of this agreement. The Advisor agrees that all such data shall remain confidential and shall not be disclosed without the prior authorization of the Client/Employer.
3. The Client/Employer hereby authorizes the Advisor to share relevant healthcare risk information about the Client/Employer's business, employees, operations, and current healthcare risk financing plans with appropriate underwriters, vendors, and suppliers, subject to all state and federal privacy regulations.
4. Any and all processes, systems, data, and material created by the Advisor under this agreement shall remain the exclusive property of the Client/Employer.
5. The Advisor shall remain an independent contractor and shall be responsible for all of his or her

Healthcare Risk Advisor Services SAMPLE AGREEMENT

own operating expenses incurred and income taxes due on the fees paid under this agreement.

6. The Client/Employer shall reimburse the Advisor for travel and other expenses incurred, subject to obtaining prior approval from the Client/Employer for those expenses.

7. Any fees due to attorneys, CPAs, or other professionals to complete any recommended projects shall fall outside the scope of this agreement and shall be the sole responsibility of the Client/Employer.

8. This agreement shall be effective (date) or such date as is mutually agreeable.

9. The fees payable under this agreement will be according to the fee structure offered below, subject to the terms of this agreement.

10. The fees payable under this agreement may be amended at any time, subject to the written agreement of the Advisor and the Client/Employer.

11. This agreement shall be for a term of 12 months and automatically renewable. The agreement may be terminated or amended by either party with 30 days' written notice.

12. Failure to pay the fees as agreed shall terminate all terms and conditions of this agreement on the last day of the month when the payment was due.

13. The Advisor shall be held harmless from any civil or criminal penalties or fines and any liabilities of the Client/Employer in connection with the legal obligations of the Client/Employer under any aspect of employment law and federal or state employment regulations.

14. In the event of termination, all fees earned through the phase of the project completed to date are due and payable.

15. This agreement shall apply in full to all successors and assignees.

16. This agreement shall be governed by the laws of the state of _____.

Fees are payable as follows:

$_____ per month due and payable on or before the 10th day of the month.

Travel expenses as preapproved.

_____   Date _____
Advisor – Name – Title

_____   Date _____
Employer – Name – Title

CHAPTER 6

The Metrics That Matter

Metrics matter. In a fee-for-services business model, your value proposition requires accurate tools and systems to measure activities, man-hours, costs, revenues, and outcomes. Those tools need to work for both the individual Healthcare Advisor and the firm. As you transition from a commission-based business model to a fee-for-services business structure, you will need to develop systems and processes to track these key performance indicators (KPIs).

As we build a set of KPIs for your advisors, staff, and firm, there are multiple data points that will need to be collected on a regular basis.

Here are a few:

1. Historical annual revenues
2. Account annual revenues
3. FTEs covered per group
4. FTEs covered for the entire firm
5. Historical total annual healthcare spend per group
6. Historical total annual healthcare spend for all groups
7. Number of groups in the firm
8. Number of groups for each advisor
9. Annual revenues per advisor
10. Compensation per advisor
11. Compensation for staff
12. Payroll burden for W-2 employees as a percent of compensation
13. Annual hours worked per advisor
14. Annual hours worked per staff
15. Total annual man-hours worked by advisors
16. Total annual man-hours worked by staff
17. Annual producer hours worked per account
18. Annual staff hours worked per account

As you transition from commissions to fee-for-services, it will take some time and effort to gather and evaluate all this information.

That raises several vital questions:

1. How do we do this?
2. Why are we doing this?
3. Where and when does all this information get applied?

How Do We Do This?

If numbers and spreadsheets are not your strength, you may need to assign data collection to someone else. However, as an advisor or the leader of your firm, you will need to understand where all the data originates and exactly what it means. Again, think of it as

The Path from Commissions to *Fee-for-Services*

a dashboard. You might need help building it and getting it wired to the right parts of the firm, but once it is operational, you will need to understand what all the dials and gauges are telling you about your performance.

Why Are We Doing This?

There are four reasons we are doing this:

1. **BENCHMARKS.** You cannot measure performance until you establish a reference point from which to measure. Benchmarks set a baseline against which performance can be measured. Professional baseball uses well-known benchmarks to measure every player's performance during each game and over the player's career. A player with a .300 batting average gets paid much more than someone with a .250 average. A .200 hitter gets replaced. Benchmarks can apply to each advisor, the firm, and each client. Benchmarks help tell a story.

2. **MILESTONES.** Think of it as measuring the forward motion and growth trajectory of the advisor and the firm. Milestones measure progress. They measure speed and trajectory. Intentionally setting milestones establishes a path for your career and your business. Without milestones, the journey will be random and unpredictable.

3. **PROFITABILITY.** You must spend money to make money. You must deploy resources—human capital, intellectual capital, relational capital, and chronological capital—to move your career and business forward. As an advisor or the leader of a firm, you need to know the most efficient and effective ways to deploy that capital to maximize revenues and earnings.

4. **PERFORMANCE-BASED COMPENSATION.** If the Healthcare Advisor enters into a performance-based compensation agreement,

> **You cannot measure performance until you establish a reference point from which to measure. Benchmarks set a baseline against which performance can be measured.**

their ultimate compensation will be based on actual plan savings. Without some benchmark of projected cost increases in the future against which to measure future savings, a performance-based compensation arrangement is not possible. (See sample Performance-Based Contract language and illustration.)

Where and When Does All This Information Get Applied?

The short answer is you may have much work to do. Some of this data will be readily available, and some will require effort to obtain. As you are gathering the data, you should also be developing processes and systems to gather the same data on an ongoing basis. Some data will apply to all activities during the year, and other metrics will be case specific. In a later chapter, we will address the issue of technology platforms to make this process easier.

Critical Benchmarks

To elaborate on the topic of benchmarks, let's go through a couple of case studies to see how benchmarking works and why it is vital to a fee-for-services business model. Benchmarking will be one of the key tools in establishing and justifying your value proposition.

Benchmarking a Group Case

Go back at least three years, and gather the following data:

1. Average number of full-time employees
2. Group benefits costs paid by employer
3. Group benefits costs paid by employees
4. Estimated current advisor income from the account

Using the data collected above, generate the following information:

1. Increase in group benefits costs over the prior two to five years
2. Increase in group benefits costs for the employer
3. Increase in group benefits costs for the employees
4. Projected increase in group benefits costs over the next three to five years
5. Items 1–4 above converted to a Per Employee Per Month (PEPM) health plan cost

In chapter 9 we will discuss in detail how to use this data and these benchmarks to support the fee-for-services model and justify your value proposition.

Benchmarking Example

Martin Construction: Historical Data *(from Group Health Plan Fact Finder)*

Employees	21 full-time employees, 18 employees enrolled in the plan
Employer contribution	75 percent of employee-only costs
1st year prior	18 full-time employees, 10 employees enrolled in the plan
2nd year prior	17 full-time employees, 11 employees enrolled in the plan
Current year costs	total: $130,000
Current year costs	employer paid: $70,000
Current year costs	employee paid: $60,000
1st year prior costs	total: $60,000
1st year prior costs	employer paid: $48,000
1st year prior costs	employee paid: $12,000
2nd years prior costs	total: $50,000
2nd years prior costs	employer paid: $37,000
2nd years prior costs	employee paid: $13,000
Estimated producer compensation	7%
Current year	$9,100
1st year prior	$4,200
2nd years prior	$3,500

The Path from Commissions to *Fee-for-Services*

Benchmarking Example (continued)

Martin Construction Benchmarks

Current total health plan cost	PEPM = $602
Current employer health plan cost	PEPM = $324
Current employee health plan cost	PEPM = $278
Current producer compensation	PEPM = $42
1 year prior total health plan cost	PEPM = $500
1 year prior employer health plan cost	PEPM = $400
1 year prior employee health plan cost	PEPM = $100
1 year prior producer compensation	PEPM = $35
2 years prior total health plan cost	PEPM = $379
2 years prior employer health plan cost	PEPM = $281
2 years prior employee health plan cost	PEPM = $98
2 years prior producer compensation	PEPM = $27

Martin Construction Conclusions

Increase in total costs	PEPM = $602 - $379 = $223 = 59%
Projected cost in 3 years from today	$956 PEPM
Projected producer compensation in 3 years	$65 PEPM

Group Health Plan Benchmark Fact Finder is available as a Word Document

Group Health Plan Benchmark Fact Finder
Fee for Services Business Plan
A transition guide for the Next-Generation Healthcare Advisor

Daniel R. Meylan   © Tapadero Partners 2019

Current Year	Total employees	_____
	Total employees on the plan	_____
	Employer contribution	_____
1st year prior	Total employees	_____
	Employees on the plan	_____
2nd year prior	Total employees	_____
	Employees on the plan	_____

Current year costs – total _____
Current year costs – employer paid _____
Current year costs – employee paid _____

1st year prior costs – total _____
1st year prior costs – employer paid _____
1st year prior costs – employee paid _____

2nd year prior costs – total _____
2nd year prior costs – employer paid _____
2nd year prior costs – employee paid _____

Estimated Producer Comp
    Current year _____
    1st year prior _____
    2nd year prior _____

Health Plan Benchmarks
    Current total PEPM _____
    Current employer PEPM _____
    Current employee PEPM _____

    Current producer comp _____

    1st year prior total PEPM _____
    1st year prior employer PEPM _____
    1st year prior employee PEPM _____
    1st year prior producer comp _____

    2nd year prior total PEPM _____
    2nd year prior employer PEPM _____
    2nd year prior employee PEPM _____
    2nd year prior producer comp _____

Benchmarking Your Fee-for-Services Next Generation Healthcare Advisory Firm

In Chapter 7, we will provide a detailed a case study on Jones & Jones Benefit Managers. For that benchmark study we gathered a number of critical metrics, including the following:

1. Total agency revenue
2. Total accounts written
3. Total FTEs covered
4. Total agency man-hours
5. Total producer man-hours

The purpose of that benchmark study was to establish an appropriate billable hourly rate that supported the value proposition of the firm and the Healthcare Advisor. Those metrics can also be utilized as benchmarks to help assess and grow the Healthcare Advisor's income and the revenue and profitability of the firm.

Setting Benchmarks for the Advisor

Dave is a Healthcare Advisor employed by Jones & Jones.

Here are Dave's key metrics:

1. Dave works 1,800 hours per year.
2. He has 27 accounts.
3. His book of business has 1,100 FTEs.
4. His book of business generates $410,000.
5. His personal income is $205,000.
6. His PEPM book average is $31.
7. His billable hourly rate is $456.

Benchmarks and Losing a Case

Dave is an experienced producer with a solid block of business who works only about 1,800 hours per year. He has not written any new business in the past two years. Dave's PEPM is lower than the agency average, but his billable hourly rate is $119 higher than the agency average. Dave's largest case with 340 lives was just sold, and Dave and the agency are about to lose $126,000 of annual income (about 31 percent of Dave's revenue). That case absorbed about fifteen hours per month, plus thirty hours at renewal, for a total of 210 hours of Dave's time during the year. Here are the critical metrics for this case:

1. $126,000 annual revenue (31 percent of Dave's income)
2. 340 lives
3. 210 hours (12 percent of Dave's time)
4. PEPM = $31
5. Billable hourly rate for this case = $600

Benchmarks and Replacing a Lost Case

To replace the $126,000 of lost income, Dave will need to choose one of the following actions:

1. Plan on devoting 275 hours next year to replacing that income (65 additional hours)
2. Set a higher billable hourly rate for the new business ($600)
3. Fnd a new case or cases with 250 lives at $42 PEPM

Benchmarking the Agency's Growth and Profitability

Solid revenue and profitability growth must be carefully planned, measured, and managed. Here is a sample dashboard from an operating agency. This is a commercial lines, personal lines, and benefits agency with 4,400 customers and $2.6 million in revenue. The agency developed detailed systems and tracked critical metrics over five years. Total revenue per person increased from $109,169 to $153,814 over five years (an increase of 41 percent). Operating profits per person increased from $5,683 to $25,841 (an increase of 455 percent).

Sample Agency

KPI Metrics Dashboard including Commissions and Fees

Sample Agency

	#1	#2	#3	#4	#5	Net Change year to year #2	#3	#4	#5
Commercial Lines									
CL Policies	1,471	1,620	1,582	1,579	1,698	149	(38)	(3)	119
CL Customers	876	945	928	928	982	69	-17	0	54
Policies/Customer	1.68	1.71	1.70	1.70	1.73	0.04	(0.01)	(0.00)	0.03
Commissions	894,651	892,744	996,273	1,021,416	1,112,380	(1,907)	103,529	25,142	90,964
Fees	99,231	112,167	124,374	153,296	173,323	12,936	12,207	28,923	20,027
Total Income	993,882	1,004,911	1,120,647	1,174,712	1,285,703	11,029	115,736	54,065	110,991
Per Policy	676	620	708	744	757	(55)	88	36	13
Per Customer	1,135	1,063	1,208	1,266	1,309	(71)	144	58	43
Personal Lines									
PL Policies	4,513	4,639	4,701	4,887	5,046	126	62	186	159
PL Customers	3,222	3,273	3,292	3,380	3,474	51	19	88	94
Policies/Customer	1.401	1.417	1.428	1.446	1.453	0.017	0.011	0.018	0.007
Commissions	919,652	909,071	989,681	1,099,256	1,155,456	(10,581)	80,611	109,575	56,200
Fees	7,832	6,315	5,810	7,990	5,625	(1,517)	(505)	2,180	(2,365)
Total Income	927,484	915,386	995,491	1,107,246	1,161,081	(12,098)	80,106	111,755	53,836
Per Policy	206	197	212	227	230	(8)	14	15	4
Per Customer	288	280	302	328	334	(8)	23	25	7
Totals									
Total Policies	5,984	6,259	6,283	6,466	6,744	275	24	183	278
Total Customers	4,098	4,218	4,220	4,308	4,456	120	2	88	148
Policies/Customer	1.460	1.484	1.489	1.501	1.513	0.024	0.005	0.012	0.013
Comm & Fee Inc	1,921,366	1,920,296	2,116,138	2,281,958	2,446,784	$ (1,069)	$ 195,842	$ 165,819	$ 164,827
Comm per Customer	469	455	501	530	549	$ (14)	$ 46	$ 28	$ 19
Total Income	2,074,206	2,051,673	2,420,592	2,380,830	2,614,830	$ (22,533)	$ 368,919	$ (39,762)	$ 234,000
Income per Customer	506	486	574	553	587	$ (20)	$ 87	$ (21)	$ 34
Total Income	2,074,206	2,051,673	2,420,592	2,380,830	2,614,830	$ (22,533)	$ 368,919	$ (39,762)	$ 234,000
Total Expenses	1,966,233	1,878,810	2,403,691	2,103,169	2,175,539	$ (87,423)	$ 524,881	$ (300,522)	$ 72,370
Operating Profit	107,973	172,863	16,901	277,661	439,291	$ 64,890	$ (155,962)	$ 260,760	$ 161,630

KPI Metrics Historical Dashboard Including Commissions & Fees

Staff	#1	#2	#3	#4	#5	Net Change year to year #2	#3	#4	#5
Producers & Staff	17	16	19	15	15	-1	3	-4	0
Contract Labor	2	2	2	2	2	0	0	0	0
Total Staff	19	18	21	17	17	-1	3	-4	0
Total Income/Person	109,169	113,982	115,266	140,049	153,814	$ 4,813	$ 1,284	$ 24,783	$ 13,765
Total Expenses/Person	103,486	104,378	114,461	123,716	127,973	$ 892	$ 10,083	$ 9,254	$ 4,257
Operating Profit/Person	5,683	9,604	805	16,333	25,841	$ 3,921	$ (8,799)	$ 15,528	$ 9,508

Notes

CHAPTER 7

What Am I Worth, Really?

What is your time worth? If you are a commissioned agent, it may not matter to you because you know that if you sell a plan, you will get paid a commission! There are four reasons that might be a problem:

1. The carrier controls the amount of commission and can change it anytime.
2. The commission might not cover your costs.
3. You might be marginalizing your professional value.
4. You are now required to fully disclose the direct and indirect (contingency) commissions you receive on you client's self-funded health plan.

Setting Your Own Billable Hourly Rate

If you are a solo advisor or an advisor inside an existing group benefits practice, it is vitally important that you know the value of your time. You need to have a clear understanding of your own billable hourly rate. Once you know the value of your time (your billable hourly rate), you can easily convert hourly rate to a contractual monthly amount or PEPM fee that reflects your time expended, resources deployed, professional expertise, and leadership delivered for each client.

Many advisors are the primary breadwinners in their households, and those households require a certain level of monthly cash flow to meet all their financial obligations. In developing an appropriate billable hourly rate for yourself, you need to ask some basic questions:

1. How many dollars does it require (in after-tax cash) to pay all the household expenses for the month?
2. How many hours a week do I work?
3. How many weeks of the year do I work?
4. Do I have a personal and business budget?
5. How many vacation days and holidays do I not work?

We have created a time-value tool that will generate a suggested billable hourly rate when the advisor inserts a series of variables. This tool also converts that billable hourly rate into a suggested PEPM fee.

It should be understood that the advisor *cannot* bill the client for business activities that are not associated directly with that group case. Here is a list of business activities that are *not* billable to a client:

1. Personal education and training
2. Business planning and marketing
3. Staff training
4. Carrier and Third Party Administrator (TPA) assessments
5. Carrier and TPA meetings and relationship building

Below is a sample of the calculation tool available as a part of my fee-for-services course. This illustrates the suggested billable hourly rate to support a household that

> This time value tool is an interactive working file that allows the variables of personal finances, payroll, burden, revenue splits with the firm (agency), time allocations, and target PEPM to be adjusted to calculate the current value of your time.
>
> This model contains certain assumptions that can be altered.
>
> 1. The revenue split between the practice and the Healthcare Advisor is 50/50.
> 2. The Healthcare Advisor can only bill a specific client for 50 percent of the actual hours worked.
> 3. Federal and state income tax loads can be adjusted.
>
> (An interactive working model of the tool is available on our website.)

Health Advisor TIME VALUE TOOL

© Daniel R Meylan (7-2009)

Household Finances

		Month	Year
How much money does it take to operate your household?		$ 7,000	$ 84,000
Deduct any sources of income other than your direct compensation		$ -	$ -
Net cash required to operate your household		$ 7,000	$ 84,000
Savings Factor (10%)		$ 700	$ 8,400
Cash required plus savings		$ 7,700	$ 92,400
Your Local, State, and Federal Taxes Burden			
FICA 6.75% Medicare 1.5% Fed Tax 12% State Tax 4%		24.25%	24.25%
Gross Pretax Income Required to Pay Household Expenses		$ 9,567	$ 114,807

Employer's Payroll Burden

FICA 6.75%	6.75%		
Medicare 1.5%	1.50%		
Workers Compensation 1.5%	1.50%		
Retirement 2.0%	2.00%		
Employee benefits 4.0%	4.00%		
Your Cost to your Employer	15.75%	$ 11,074	$ 132,889
Book of Business @50%		$ 22,148	$ 265,778

Time

How many hours per day do you work?			9.0
How many days per week do you work?			5.0
Total hours per year			2,340
How many days (hours) of vacation do you take?		10	(90)
How many legal holidays (hours) do you observe (the post office is closed)		9	(81)
Total Hours Worked in a Year			2,169

Your Value per Hour

Your hourly cost to your employer		$ 61
Net take-home hourly income including savings		$ 43
Your hourly value to your employer		$ 123
Your Billable Rate to your Client (x2)		$ 245

Covered Employees Required

PEPM	Covered
$ 25	886
$ 30	738
$ 40	554

© Daniel R Meylan (7-2009)
(Modified for Fee for Services Training 6-1-2019)
Tapadero Partners, LLC
dmeylan@weaversonline.org
719-338-6466

Chapter 7: *What Am I Worth, Really?*

requires $7,000 per month to operate. This producer works nine hours a day, five days a week, with ten days of vacation and nine legal holidays. His or her suggested billable hourly rate would be $245 per hour or $30 PEPM for a block of business with 738 covered FTEs.

Setting the Billable Hourly Rate for the Agency or the Practice

As an agency or practice principal, what is the value of time for your firm? Do you care whether your agency is adequately compensated by the commissions you receive for the work you do on the group health plans? Chances are good that if you are reading this material, you believe you are not getting adequately compensated by some clients and you now recognize that there is a federal law that requires your firm and your healthcare advisors to fully disclose all direct and indirect compensation including any contingent income!

Therefore, if you are going to enter into a fee-for-services agreement with your group clients, how are you going to set an appropriate billable hourly rate for your agency or practice? How are you going to establish the value of your agency time and be able to justify that rate?

Once you begin looking for that answer, you quickly realize that there are additional questions that need to be addressed:

1. What is the billable rate for producers?
2. What is the billable rate for staff?
3. When can we charge our clients a fee?
4. What activities performed within an agency are not billable?

In answering these questions, you will need to gather some important data about the operations of your agency. This data will be the foundational information you use to establish

> **Establishing the billable hourly rate for the Healthcare Advisor group benefits practice will be the cornerstone of your larger budgeting process.**

and monitor the hourly fee-for-services billing rate.

1. The number of man-hours worked by each person in the agency in the year
2. The amount of revenue each producer generates
3. The number of cases written
4. The number of full-time employees in each group and in total

Most agents and firms do not have this information readily available. Your first assignment will be to take the time to gather this critical data. Make sure the data you collect is as accurate as possible.

Before we look at a case study, we need to discuss exactly how an advisor spends his or her work time during the year. Why is this important? As stated above about the individual advisor, the agency or practice *cannot* bill a client for business activities that are not associated directly with that group case. Here is a list of agency or firm business activities that are not billable to a client:

1. Advisor and staff education and training
2. Business planning and marketing
3. Carrier and TPA assessments
4. Carrier and TPA meetings and relationship building

5. Compliance training
6. Industry association involvement
7. Political involvement
8. Volunteer work
9. Routine business management work

Setting the Billable Hourly Rate for the Firm

If you are the principal, ask yourself this question: *How much revenue do we need in order to meet our corporate financial objectives while compensating our staff well, financing our future growth, and generating a profit?*

For comparison, you might ask, *What is a comparable hourly billing rate for a local CPA or law firm?* Hourly billing rates vary dramatically and are certainly not the same in New York or Washington, DC, as in Edmond, Oklahoma, or Lubbock, Texas.

Establishing the billable hourly rate for the Healthcare Advisor group benefits practice will be the cornerstone of your larger budgeting process. Several methods and processes can be used to set your target annual revenue:

1. Use the historical annualized commission-based income as a starting point and apply appropriate growth factors to set a target annual revenue.
2. Select a target annualized gross revenue figure based on projected costs plus profits and taxes.

Nonbillable Hours

When establishing a billable hourly rate, you cannot bill a client for 100 percent of each advisor's time. Based on my forty-eight-plus years of agency operations and advisor sales management, I believe you should be able to bill at least 50 percent of an advisor's time to a specific client or employer.

The formula for establishing a billable hourly rate looks like this:

> *Annual Target Revenue ÷ Total Advisor Man-Hours x 2*

Billable Hours Case Study

We will assume that 50 percent of the annual hours worked by the Health Advisor can be billed to a specific client. Here is an example:

Jones & Jones Benefit Managers

Principals	2 (1 full-time; 1 semi-retired)
Producers	3 (2 full-time; 1 part-time)
Staff	4 (3 full-time; 1 part-time)
Group Cases	108
FTE employees covered by all group plans	2,674
Annual revenue	$1,445,000
Annual compensation for all producers and staff	$650,000
Principals' base compensation	$300,000
Payroll burden	$180,000
Occupancy & admin	$165,000
Average PEPM (per employee, per month) revenue	$45.03

Notes

CHAPTER 8

Transparent, Balanced Compensation

Now that we have introduced metrics, let's explore how they can be applied to performance-based fee-for-services compensation. This compensation methodology ties the income of the advisor directly to his or her ability to bring a measurable improved outcome to the group client.

Some basic criteria must be defined to even begin a discussion about performance-based fee-for-services compensation.

The ideal client/employer would:
1. Employ fifty or more FTEs;
2. Provide accurate data on historical health plan costs;
3. Nurture a culture that values collaboration and an educational approach to managing healthcare risk (rather than simply looking for the lowest cost);
4. Display strong support and buy-in from ownership and management;
5. Embrace the operational change and cultural shifts required to improve their bottom line;
6. Be willing to execute a long-term advisor agreement that includes the specific metrics that will drive the Healthcare Advisor's performance compensation;
7. Provide you, the advisor, the opportunity to reduce overall plan costs by a meaningful percentage.

Note: Go/No-Go Decisions

After you have determined the characteristics of your ideal performance-based client, you have the basis for a go/no-go decision about any new case opportunity. If the prospect does not meet your basic criteria, move on. Do not waste your valuable time and resources or attempt to work on a performance-based compensation arrangement with less-than-ideal clients.

A Sample Performance-Based Fee-for-Services Compensation Case Study

- A private school (K–12)
- 135 FTEs – 110 enrolled
- 2017 current plan – fully insured (carrier: BUCAH)
- 2017 expiring costs = $900,000 ($682 PEPM)
- 2017 employee deductibles and copays = $169 PEPM
- 2018 fully insured renewal proposal = $1,062,000 ($805 PEPM)
- 2018–19 Healthcare Advisor performance-based fee-for-services proposal: **$15 PEPM + 20% of any reduction in cost from expiring plan**

New Plan 2018
- Partially self-funded – $50,000 SPEC
- Direct primary care for all FTEs paid by employer
- Direct primary care managing chronic illnesses and dispensing meds at cost
- Reference-based pricing network
- Transparent PBM (pharmacy benefit manager) flat fee only – all rebates back to employer

Results
- 85% of FTEs and family enrolled with a DPC
- DPC costs = $105,000 ($80 PEPM)
- Fixed costs for TPA = $81,000
- Stop-loss costs = $161,000
- Claims costs paid by plan = $290,000
- Net plan savings = $263,000 (Rx spending was reduced by 65%)
- Net savings in employee deductibles and copays = $132,000 ($100 PEPM)
- Healthcare Advisor performance bonus = $52,600
- Healthcare Advisor base fee = $19,800
- Healthcare Advisor total compensation = $72,400 ($55 PEPM)

After paying the Healthcare Advisor's bonus fee, this private school had an additional $210,400 to put toward other operational costs including salaries and funding for special needs students. It should also be noted that the advisor made a substantial donation back to the school from his earned bonus. At renewal, the advisor and the senior management of the school used the detailed claims data provided by the DPC, TPA, and PBM to establish strategies to reduce costs in the next year even further. Both the TPA and the stop-loss carrier reduced their costs at renewal. The advisor maintained his original performance-based fee-for-services agreement.

Public Entity
Five-Year Performance-Based Compensation Proposal Case Study

Below is a summary of the employee benefits costs for a county. Note the key metrics identified in this summary.

Year	2016	2017	2018	2019	2020
Annual Budget	$43,000,000	$49,200,000	$51,350,000	$53,000,000	$51,000,000
Total FTEs	421	444	441	451	438
Total FTEs on the Plan	126	151	133	152	155
Total Lives	221	264	233	266	271
Total Plan Costs	$619,920	$770,100	$796,404	$957,600	$1,106,700
PEPM Plan Costs	$410.00	$425.00	$499.00	$525.00	$595.00
Annual Increase	0.00%	3.66%	17.41%	5.21%	3.33%
Cumulative Increase	0.00%	3.66%	21.07%	26.28%	39.61%
% of Budget	1.44%	1.44%	1.55%	1.81%	2.17%

The PEPM costs for the county increased from $410 to $595 (or 45%) over five years, but more important was the increase as a percentage of the total operating budget. Their cost as a percentage of budget increased from 1.47% to 2.17%. If the rate of increase for their health plan over the next five years mirrored the increases from the prior five years, the projected cost of their health plan in five years would be 2.92% of the budget or almost $1.5M annually. This was unacceptable to the county leadership who were actively seeking ways to reduce plan costs and improve member experience.

Year	2021	2022	2023	2024	2025
Annual Budget	$51,000,000	$51,000,000	$51,000,000	$51,000,000	$51,000,000
Total FTEs					
Total FTEs on the Plan	155	155	155	155	155
Total Lives					
Total Plan Costs	$1,175,520	$1,244,340	$1,313,160	$1,381,980	$1,450,80
PEPM Plan Costs	$632.00	$669.00	$706.00	$743.00	$780.00
Annual Increase					
Cumulative Increase					
% of Budget	2.32%	2.47%	2.62%	2.77%	2.92%

The Path from Commissions to *Fee-for-Services*

Public Entity (continued)
Five-Year Performance-Based Compensation Proposal Case Study

The advisor offered suggestions for possible solutions to reduce cost and improve member experience. The county leadership embraced the idea that this advisor would be willing to accept a perfomance-based compensation arrangement.

The performance-based agreement offered by the advisor included:
1. Base compensation of $15 PEPM to be billed monthly.
2. Complete transparency on all compensation received by the advisor for ancillary products.
3. Established and contractually agreed to benchmark reference points for calculation of future-based performance-based compensation for five years.
4. Performance-based compensation fee of 20% of the net savings for each plan year measured against the agreed-upon benchmarks in #3 above.

Based on the proposed performance-based compensation and the assumption that the advisor would successfully hold the overall plan costs flat (average performance) through year #2, below is a representation of the advisor's performance-based revenue in year #2.

However, if the advisor and their team successfully reduced the overall cost of the county's plan to $900,000 in year #2, their performance-based compensation would increase by over $40K or more than 60%.

Performance-Based Compensation Model **Average Performance**	
Year	2022
FTEs	155
Base Fee	$15.00
Benchmark Target	$1,244,340
Actual Cost	$1,106,700
Ancillary PEPM	$4.75
Base Fee	$27,900
Ancillary Fee	$8,835
Performance Bonus	$27,528
Total Comp	$64,263
PEPM Equivilant	35

Performance-Based Compensation Model **Superior Performance**	
Year	2022
FTEs	155
Base Fee	$15.00
Benchmark Target	$1,244,340
Actual Cost	$900,000
Ancillary PEPM	$4.75
BaseFee	$27,900
Ancillary Fee	$8,835
Performance Bonus	$68,868
Total Comp	$105,603
PEPM Equivilant	57

(This addendum is offered as a sample of what a performance-based agreement might include. There are many ways to structure performance-based compensation. This illustration DOES NOT address all the variables that might impact a performance-based compensation agreement.)

Fee-for-Services Healthcare Risk Advisor Services Agreement

Exhibit A
Performance-Based Compensation Addendum

This contract addendum shall serve as an agreement for the compensation to be paid by the "client" to the "advisor" for the services rendered by the "advisor" under this agreement.

Whereas the "client" desires to reduce the costs of their healthcare plan while improving the quality of healthcare services and improving the member experience for their plan members and;

Whereas the "client' is willing to enter into a performance-based compensation agreement that will reward the "advisor" for reducing overall plan costs and;

Whereas the "advisor" is confident that they can reduce plan costs and improve the plan member's experience and;

Whereas the "advisor" is willing to enter into a performance-based compensation agreement based on future plan cost reductions and the improved value of the "client's" self-funded group health plan.

It is now agreed that the "advisor" shall be compensated under this agreement as follows:

BASE Compensation $_____ PEPM

PERFORMANCE COMPENSATION

_____% of the reduction in the PEPM costs as determined and agreed to by the "client" based on the review and analysis of the PEPM plan costs prepared by the **"cost of risk study"** prepared by the "advisor" and certified by the client.

The percentage of the saving performance bonus shall be applied to the reduction in current plan costs against the projected costs as determined by the **"cost of risk study."**

Definition "Cost of Risk Study". The cost of risk study shall be an in-depth review of plan costs over the prior ____ years to determine the projected cost increase over the next ____ years should the client retain their current plan structure and design.

Fee-for-Services Healthcare Risk Advisor Services Agreement *(continued)*

Performance-Based Compensation Model

Example:

Model Assumptions

Base Comp	$ 15 PEPM
Performance Comp	20% of net reductions
Current year FTEs	220

Cost of Risk Study Results

Year	Plan Costs	Net Increase
5 years prior	$ 421 PEPM	
4 years prior	$ 444 PEPM	
3 years prior	$ 522 PEPM	
2 years prior	$ 571 PEPM	
Current year	$ 655 PEPM	56% over 5 years
Historical annual increase	6%	

Future Results Performance-Based Compensation Outcome

Projected Increase @ 6% per year

Upcoming year	$ 695 PEPM
Next year	$ 737 PEPM
Following year	$ 781 PEPM

Performance-Based Calculation Example

Projected upcoming year costs	$ 695 PEPM
Performance Bonus agreement	20% of savings
Actual plan costs	$ 575 PEPM
Net savings	$ 120 PEPM
Bonus earned (20% of savings)	$ 24 PEPM

Base Comp	**$ 15 PEPM**
Base Comp and Bonus	**$ 39 PEPM**
Plan Savings after Advisor Comp	**$ 96**
Plan Cost Savings	**$ 253,440**
Total Advisor Revenue	**$ 102,960**

CHAPTER 9

Closing and Locking the Door— Selling Your Fee-for-Services Value Proposition

For those who have always worked for a commission and never actually established and communicated a value proposition beyond being a "health insurance broker," this next step may seem intimidating. It is only as difficult as you make it. If you prepare properly, you will be successful. You might be surprised how easy it is if you approach the process correctly—with the right attitude and strategy.

First, you should know and be able to clearly communicate your value proposition. If you are still unclear about exactly what your value proposition is, go back to chapters 2 and 3 and review that material.

This is what your perspective should be: *We are worth what we are charging because of the value we bring to our employer clients.*

This is what your message should be: *We can justify our fees by the value we bring to your company and your employees.* (State this in your own language.)

The most critical first step in selling your value proposition is this: know your decision-maker! Before you suggest your fee-for-services plan, understand the leadership and behavior style of the primary decision-maker. (Of course, be sure you are talking to the primary decision-maker.)

Learn as much as you can about the following:

1. How strong a leader is this person?
2. Will he or she be resistant to change?
3. Does this person have any pain surrounding his or her current plan and processes?
4. Does he or she understand healthcare risk management processes?
5. Will this person put an appropriate value on your value proposition?
6. Will this decision-maker understand and appreciate your economic value?

Ultimately every sale hinges on three critical components, which we call "the three-legged stool of sales."

The Path from Commissions to *Fee-for-Services*   57

> *"Arrogance always magnifies ignorance."*
> —Daniel Meylan

Wisdom (not intelligence) is the hallmark of great leadership!

Intelligence or Wisdom?

- *Intelligence talks.*
  Wisdom listens.
- *Intelligence thinks.*
  Wisdom knows.
- *Intelligence knows the answer.*
  Wisdom knows the question.
- *Intelligence knows what.*
  Wisdom knows why.
- *Intelligence hears it all.*
  Wisdom listens to what is not said.
- *Intelligence knows the mind.*
  Wisdom knows the heart.
- *Intelligence counts.*
  Wisdom cares.
- *Intelligence works.*
  Wisdom wins.

The Product, the Process, and the Politics

The product and process are always technical but are not that difficult. When a sales process fails, it usually does so because of the politics behind the sale, not the product or process. Advisors operating on a fee-for-services basis must always focus first on the key relationships that drive all aspects of the client's decision-making and plan execution. Successful advisors always focus first on building strong relationships with *all* the key decision-makers, not just the CEO, CFO, or HR director.

Maybe the best way to determine whether you have the right type of business owner / decision-maker is to describe someone who is *not* a candidate for your fee-for-services value proposition.

The noncandidate:

1. Is an egotistical and arrogant leader;
2. Is a poor listener;
3. Places little, if any, value on the employees;
4. Sees employee benefits as a liability;
5. Resents and patronizes;
6. Bids all purchases every time;
7. Is a short-term, lowest-cost, price-driven client;
8. Displays marginal operational business competence;
9. Lacks a collaborative decision-making style.

Take the opposite of each of these noncandidate characteristics, and you will most likely have a strong candidate for a fee-for-services proposal.

The Fee-for-Services Script

Since most of the Healthcare Advisors using this workbook have a substantial amount of commission-based business, the primary questions are these:

1. How do we go about introducing our fee-for-services concept to existing clients who currently pay for our services through commissions?
2. How do we introduce our Healthcare Advisor fee-for-services value proposition to a new client?

In both cases, the script is similar but may need to be adapted according to the nature of your relationship. Do not assume that your current commission-based clients are not open to considering a fee-for-services approach.

Start by reviewing all your current commission-based clients by asking, "Is this client a candidate for fee-for-services based on the criteria discussed in the prior paragraphs?"

Next prepare a script for each type of presentation. Here are two sample scripts. These are suggested scripts only. You can modify them to fit your style and personality and the nature of your relationship with your prospective or current client (see the next two pages for script examples).

SCRIPT 1: Yes!

This group is a candidate for a fee-for-services agreement.

(This script assumes you have access to the details about this group's health plan costs over the past five years.)

Start with questions to the primary decision-maker. I always like to start with questions because they give the employer (decision-maker) the opportunity to respond and engage.

---

1. Are you aware that annual healthcare spending in America now exceeds $11,000 per person?

2. Are you aware that almost twenty cents of every dollar made in America today is being spent on healthcare?

3. Are you aware of how much the cost of your group health plan has increased over the past five years?

4. Are you aware of how much of your operating revenues go to your group health plan?

5. What do you think will happen with the cost of your group health plan over the next five years?

6. If your health plan costs increase over the next five years at the same pace they increased over the last five years, will you be able to offer a group health plan?

7. Are you aware that the healthcare conditions within your group ultimately determine the cost of the health plan for both you and the employees?

8. Are you aware that the No Surprises Act passed by Congress in 2019 requires that brokers now fully disclose any direct or indirect commissions received on your group health plan?

We would like to propose a new approach that manages the healthcare risk within your group health plan to make sure you can continue to offer an affordable health plan for your employees well into the future.

We are applying to be your Healthcare Advisor. As your Healthcare Advisor, our role is to help you control the cost of the healthcare risk within your group. Since 80 percent of the cost of insurance plans is driven directly by the cost of claims, we are proposing a process that will help you aggressively manage the cost of claims—not just offer a low-cost bid for your group health plan

Unfortunately, insurance alone is not the answer. Today, insurance carriers offer few, if any, options that effectively reduce the cost of healthcare risk. Their systems are antiquated and self-serving, and their cost-control services are marginal. They do not really compete for your business. Managing healthcare risk today involves much more than just buying a group health insurance plan.

We would like to enter into a formal contract with you that will specify the healthcare risk management services we will offer. This agreement will include specific deliverables that are mutually agreeable, along with provisions for transparent fees in lieu of commissions and termination clauses if we fail to meet the contract terms. This contract will also require certain actions on your part to enable us to complete our portion of the agreement. As a final component of our agreement, we are willing to offer a performance-based compensation plan that is not tied to commissions but rewards us as we successfully reduce your costs and improve your member experience.

If you have an interest in retaining us as your Healthcare Advisor, we would like to provide a sample Healthcare Advisor risk agreement for your review.

SCRIPT 2: No!

This group does not appear to be a candidate for a fee-for-services agreement. Start with these questions.

---

1. Are you aware that annual healthcare spending in America now exceeds $11,000 per person?

2. Are you aware that almost twenty cents of every dollar made in America today is being spent on healthcare?

3. Are you aware of how much the cost of your group health plan has increased over the past five years?

4. Are you aware of how much of your operating revenues go to your group health plan?

5. What do you think will happen with the cost of your group health plan over the next five years?

6. If your health plan costs increase over the next five years at the same pace they increased over the last five years, will you be able to offer a group health plan?

7. Are we correct in assuming you still want to just bid your group insurance plan over the next five years and not consider any other options to control your costs?

8. Are you aware that the No Surprises Act passed by Congress in 2019 requires that brokers now fully disclose any direct or indirect commissions received on your group health plan?

Would you like to consider a different approach that manages the healthcare risk within your group health plan to make sure you can continue to offer an affordable health plan for your employees well into the future?

This new approach replaces the insurance broker with a Healthcare Advisor. A Healthcare Advisor helps you control the cost of the healthcare risk within your group. Since 80 percent of the cost of insurance plans is driven directly by the cost of claims, this new approach helps you aggressively manage the cost of claims. This process does not just bid your insurance in the hope that it will keep costs lower.

Bidding insurance is not the answer. Today, insurance carriers offer few, if any, options that effectively reduce the cost of healthcare risk. Their systems are antiquated and self-serving, and their cost-control services are marginal. They do not really compete for your business. Managing healthcare risk today involves much more than bidding out insurance plans.

A Healthcare Advisor offers a contract that specifies the healthcare risk management services they will offer. **This agreement includes specific deliverables that are mutually agreeable, along with provisions for transparent fees in lieu of commissions and termination clauses if the advisor fails to meet the contract terms.** This contract requires certain actions on your part to enable the Healthcare Advisor to complete the agreement. The final component of the agreement is a performance-based compensation plan that is not tied to commissions but rewards the advisor for successfully reducing your costs and improving your member experience.

Would you be interested in seeing an example of a Healthcare Advisor risk agreement?

Notes

CHAPTER 10

Signatures Matter—*Closing the Deal*

The employer said, yes, they would like to retain you as their Healthcare Advisor. Now what? You will have to finalize an agreement that is acceptable to both you and the employer.

Preparation

Here are several key points to help you prepare:

1. Discover. What are this employer's objectives, and how much of your time and resources will it take to achieve their objectives? Make sure you understand the scope of the deliverables required to meet the employer's objectives.
2. Be flexible. Recognize that the employer sees you and your solutions differently than you do. Be prepared to adjust. Contracts are much more flexible than commissions. Be creative.
3. Be prepared to start small and work up to a larger fee and time commitment as the employer sees the value of your work, or offer a performance-based compensation package.
4. Be prepared to discuss the metrics (time and money) involved with the selected deliverables.
5. Prepare your entire scope of services for the employer to review. Let them select the services they think they need.
6. Be prepared to compare your services with those of a traditional broker. How many of the services you are proposing is their current broker delivering?
7. Be prepared to discuss your value proposition and the benefit of fees versus commissions. *Do not* sell your time for less than it is worth!
8. If compensation is to be based on performance, set up the appropriate metrics against which performance will be measured. How and when will performance-based compensation be calculated and paid?

Negotiation

Review your complete scope of services with the employer and answer any questions.

1. Know your billable hourly rate. Know your target PEPM rate. (See chapters 6 and 7 if you need further information.)
2. Negotiate the contract as an annual commitment, payable in equal monthly payments.
3. Negotiate the contract as automatically renewable with a provision that the client may terminate after one year according to the contract termination conditions.
4. Allow for contract addendums so changes can be made to the scope of services and to allow for growth in the size and complexity of the group plan.
5. Fully disclose any additional fees or commissions being earned.
6. Include a proposed performance-based compensation addendum to the contract.
7. Support plan members as needed in obtaining the best possible medical outcomes at the most favorable financial terms for the plan.

Execution

Have the employer select the scope of services and initial each service they are selecting.

1. Make any requested changes to the provisions of the contract.
2. Execute the agreement with two original copies, one for the employer and one for the agency.
3. Deliver a project list that offers deliverables and timelines for designated projects.
4. Set up a specific line of communication in order to effectively communicate responsibilities to all parties and stakeholders.

Documentation

1. Set up a system to send invoices and collect fee payments per the contract. Be sure systems are in place to manage delinquent payments.
2. Document all telephone, email, snail mail, or text communications with the employer and their employees and with carriers or TPAs on behalf of the employer.
3. Create an activity log for the employer that tracks time involved (see the discussion of technology platforms in chapter 11).
4. Preschedule periodic employer meetings to execute the deliverables per the scope of services in the agreement.
5. Prepare periodic reports on the status of the projects and key performance indicators (KPIs).
6. Deliver as agreed:
    a. Detailed claims reports
    b. Performance compensation reports
    c. Regulatory and compliance updates

CHAPTER 11

Systematize Your Operation—
No Loose Ends

Great businesses are built on great systems.

In the transition to a fee-for-services business model, having sound, efficient operating systems and processes will be critical. Any business built with marginal operating systems will struggle. Every aspect of business operations needs to be systematized.

Systems accomplish tasks, produce measurable and meaningful results, and track and deliver critical operational and financial information. Systems should do the following:

- Enable people
- Seamlessly facilitate the deliverables of the business
- Maximize productivity

Systems are more than just technology platforms that manage data. Technology is a tool, like a hammer or a saw. In the hands of a skilled craftsman, it becomes productive. In the hands of an untrained or careless person, tools are ineffective at best and dangerous at worst. Systems are behavior maps that allow all the

"Great businesses are built on great systems."
—*Daniel Meylan*

Business Systems

- Finance and accounting
- Distribution
- Purchasing
- Product ordering, handling, and delivery
- Sales, customer service, and satisfaction
- Information management
- Marketing
- Computers and technology
- Physical plant, tools, equipment, and vehicles
- Human resources

The Path from Commissions to *Fee-for-Services*

> **The challenge will be to design and build a collection of systems and processes that serves the unique needs of your business model.**

stakeholders to work effectively and efficiently to fulfill their responsibilities and achieve the desired outcomes of the Healthcare Advising (CRM) firm and their customers.

These are the critical systems in a fee-for-services business plan:

1. Finance and accounting
2. Client relationship management
3. Human resources (time and productivity measures)
4. Enrollment and HR data management
5. Claim reporting and communication
6. Marketing and sales
7. Regulatory and compliance
8. Web-based client portals including apps
9. Cybersecurity

Unfortunately, there is no single technology platform that offers all these system disciplines in one application. There are technology platforms that offer solutions in multiple areas, but to the best of our knowledge, there are none that meet every requirement your fee-for-services business model will have.

The challenge will be to design and build a collection of systems and processes that serve the unique needs of your business model, your value proposition, and your customer base. You may need to build your own systems for certain areas—for example, to measure the man-hours spent servicing a specific client.

Here are some suggestions for each area of currently available technology and notes on where you may have to build your own. This is not an exhaustive list; there are many more than we have listed here.

1. Finance and accounting: AgencyBloc, QuickBooks
2. Client relationship management: HR360, Employee Navigator, Ease
3. Human resources (time and productivity measures): build your own
4. Data management: AgencyBloc, HR360, Ease, FormFire
5. Claims reporting: TPA claims platforms
6. Communications: Outlook, various email platforms
7. Marketing and sales: AgencyBloc, Salesforce, FormFire
8. Regulatory and compliance: HR360, Employee Navigator
9. Web-based client portals including apps: various or customized
10. Cybersecurity: Zix, Barracuda

Be aware that the major insurance carriers are making multi billion-dollar investments in technology platforms that will enable them to manage member and group data and communicate directly with plan members. Many of these systems will bypass the agent, and it is a simple matter for these carriers to limit the Healthcare Advisor's access to client information. Also, these carriers view the employer's claims data as their proprietary data and rarely provide detailed claims data to the group or advisor.

Specifically, in the small group and individual markets, these technology platforms will enable the major carriers to deal directly with members and either reduce or eliminate the Healthcare Advisor's involvement and justify the reduction or elimination of commissions.

The Healthcare Advisor firm operating on a fee-for-services model will need to match or exceed the systems and technology capabilities of the major carriers.

Errors and Omissions Policies and Fee-for-Services

If you are going to operate under the fee-for-services agreement, it is vitally important that you read and understand your errors and omissions policy before you have an error and omissions claim. Just because you receive a legal notice that you have violated a regulation or a client is planning to make a claim against you for failure to perform does not mean that your E&O policy is going to respond. Usually when you notify your E&O carrier of a possible claim, you will receive what is called a reservation-of-rights letter.

A reservation-of-rights letter is provided by your E&O carrier and indicates that a claim may or may not be covered under your policy. A reservation-of-rights letter does not deny a claim. However, the letter indicates that the insurer is investigating the claim and reserves the right to deny the claim after they complete their investigation.

A reservation-of-rights letter can appear generic but is a formal indicator that while the insurance company is moving forward with a claim, some losses may not be covered. The insurance carrier cannot maintain their reservation of rights indefinitely. You can usually push for their decision to provide or deny coverage, but they typically will not render a decision until they have completed a full investigation.

The standard health insurance agent's errors and omissions policy provides limited coverage for fee-for-services consulting and may not cover all the service being rendered in your fee-for-services contract with the employer. Prior to offering a fee-for-services agreement, the Healthcare Advisor should review their current errors and omissions policy and either modify the existing contract or acquire an additional errors and omissions policy to cover the scope of services being offered within the fee-for-services agreement.

Here is an example of the standard wording in a traditional life and health insurance agent's E&O policy. Please take notice of the basic insuring agreement; the definitions of *wrongful act*, *professional services*, and *covered product*; and the detailed policy exclusions.

Abridged Sample of an Insurance Agent's E&O Policy

(This review of policy language is intended as an illustration only and not a full disclosure of an entire insurance agent's errors and omissions insurance contract. Actual contracts vary and should be reviewed carefully by the policyholders.)

The company shall pay on behalf of an insured all damage which the insured becomes legally obligated to pay by reason of any wrongful act. Coverage shall apply only to such claims arising out of the insured's professional services.

Wrongful act means any actual or alleged error, misstatement, misleading statement, neglect, or breach of duty by the insured in the rendering of or failure to render professional services.

Professional services means the following:

Services by an insured for a client in the conduct of the named insured's profession as a life and/or accident and health insurance agent or insurance consultant.

1. Soliciting (whether directly or indirectly), negotiating, placing, recommending, selling, or servicing a covered product; but not including the sale, surrender, conversion, or alteration of a covered product in order to acquire or invest in anything other than a covered product.
2. Providing advice or consultation solely related to a covered product, including financial planning or consulting solely related to a covered product; but not including any advice or recommendation to, in any way, sell, surrender, convert, or alter a covered product in order to acquire or invest in anything other than a covered product.
3. Assisting a client to secure premium financing from a licensed premium finance company for a covered product placed by or on behalf of the insured.
4. Training, managing, and supervising others but only in connection with covered products.
5. Providing expert witness testimony related to professional services or a covered product.

Covered product means the following products offered, sold, or serviced in the conduct of the named insured's profession:

1. Fixed life insurance, accident and health insurance, Medicare supplement insurance, disability income insurance, or fixed annuities
2. Equity-indexed annuities
3. Variable life and variable annuity products
4. Mutual funds, investment advisor or investment advisor representative
5. Long-term care insurance
6. Group employee benefit plans (other than a *multiple employer welfare arrangement*, as that term is defined in the Employee Retirement Income Security Act of 1974 [ERISA], as amended), such as Section 125 plans, group life plans, group accident and health plans, group long-term care plans, and group disability plans, provided such plans are fully insured or are self-insured and subject to stop-loss coverage or reinsurance at all times
7. Retirement, pension, or profit-sharing plans
8. Property and casualty insurance
9. Workers' compensation insurance
10. Fidelity and surety bonds

Abridged Sample of an Insurance Agent's E&O Policy (continued)

The most important part of any insurance contract is the exclusions. Here is a brief summary of standard exclusions you can expect to see in most insurance agent E&O policies. Please note that this contract excludes any damages involving violation of ERISA and any welfare or benefit plan. Please review the exclusions of your current E&O policy carefully prior to entering into a fee-for-services agreement.

Exclusions

This insurance does not apply to the following:

A. Abuse or molestation
B. Bankruptcy or nonpayment
C. Bodily injury or property damage
D. Class-action claims
E. Confidential or personally identifiable information disclosure
F. Contractual liability
G. Criminal, fraudulent, malicious, dishonest, or intentional acts
H. Employment-related practices
I. ERISA: any damages for which any insured is liable because of liability imposed on a fiduciary by the Employee Retirement Income Security Act of 1974 (ERISA) and its amendments or by any similar federal, state, or local law
J. Fungi
K. Improper use of funds
L. Insured versus insured
M. Intellectual property infringement
N. Investments and securities
O. Management and disposition of assets
P. Market fluctuation
Q. Pension, welfare, or benefit plans of an insured or any pension, welfare, or benefit plan organized for the benefit of employees of an insured
R. Pollution
S. Prior acts, prior knowledge, or prior notice
T. Structured settlements
U. Tax, securities, and financial
V. Third-party claims administration or public claims services
W. Violation of statutes
X. Warranties

Some healthcare consultants' errors and omissions policies contemplate fee-for-services exposures. The primary differences between a healthcare consultant's E&O policy and a standard insurance agent's E&O policy are how they define *professional services and the policy exclusions*. Here is an abridged sample of an E&O policy for a healthcare consultant.

Abridged Sample of a Healthcare Consultant's E&O Policy

Wrongful act means any actual or alleged error or omission committed solely in the performance of or failure to perform professional services.

Professional services means only those services performed for others for a fee which are listed in item 6 of the declarations, provided, however, professional services shall not include medical services or legal services. [In this case, the term *healthcare consulting* would appear on the declarations page under item 6, and a more complete definition of *healthcare consulting* would be endorsed on the policy.]

Professional Services Exclusions

No coverage shall be available under this policy for any claim based upon, arising out of, directly or indirectly resulting from, in consequence of, or in any way involving:

(1) any criminal, fraudulent, dishonest, or discriminatory act

Insured may be held liable:

    (a) Under any workers' compensation law

    (b) For damage to or destruction of any tangible property

    (c) For any injury or damage arising out of aircraft, auto, or watercraft

(2) Any actual or alleged infringement of patent, etc.

(3) Any act involving an insured's fiduciary obligation as an employer or benefit plan sponsor; any certified auditing, accounting, architectural, or engineering services; or any advice relating to mergers or acquisitions

(4) Any action brought by any federal, state, or local governmental, regulatory, or administrative agency

(5) Any actual or alleged employment practices

(6) Any act, error, or omission under any prior policy

Fee-for-Services Benefits Plan State-Specific Compliance

This is just a quick warning to make yourself aware of the insurance regulations in the state where you intend to offer a fee-for-services agreement to a client. Each state has their own statutes and regulations regarding fee-for-services as it relates to health insurance products and services.

Some states are silent or have minimal statutes or regulations. Some states' statutes are specific and require certification and licensing. Some states allow commission and fee-for-services consulting arrangements to coexist; other states prohibit charging fees and commissions at the same time.

The prevailing concept is, regardless of regulatory jurisdiction, you must have a written agreement with your client to have a legitimate fee-for-services contract. If that contract fully discloses all the terms and conditions that apply, as well as the fees to be charged, and if the client has signed the contract and agreed to the terms, the agreement is valid and enforceable.

Any specific statute or regulation that might apply in your state should be included in your basic fee-for-services agreement.

Also, it is vitally important that your fee-for-services agreement should be reviewed by competent legal counsel to confirm you are not in violation of a state or federal regulation or statute.

Perpetuation

A commission-based insurance practice always has a strong asset value and can be sold to a willing buyer at a multiple of earnings. The question is, *Would a fee-for-services consulting practice specializing in group health plans have the same market value as a commission-based insurance agency?*

> **Any specific statute or regulation that might apply in your state should be included in your basic agreement.**

The answer is dependent on six factors:
1. The quality and effectiveness of the foundational systems and process in the fee-for-services practice
2. The quality and duration of the existing fee-for-services agreements
3. The expertise of the staff and advisors
4. The contractual employment relationship between the staff and advisors and the practice
5. The relationship between the buyer and the practice
6. The motivation and resources of the buyer

A fee-for-services practice may have a higher market value if all six factors are positive. An immature, marginally profitable fee-for-services practice will have minimal market value. A mature, well-managed fee-for-services practice, with solid operating systems and a track record of consistent growth and profitability, will always have exceptional market value.

Notes

CHAPTER 12

What's Next?

The one consistent reality in our world is change—unpredictable, unrelenting change.

The COVID-19 pandemic has proved that. When it comes to change, there are three types of business leaders:

1. The survivors, who react to change
2. The successful, who anticipate change
3. The significant, who drive change

If you have any desire to make a significant impact in the healthcare marketplace, you need to be committed to driving change! You cannot afford to generate change while allowing someone else to determine the value of your leadership and professionalism.

Commissions on group health insurance products are no longer adequate to appropriately compensate the true Healthcare Advisor. There is already strong evidence that commission amounts paid by carriers will continue to diminish and may be eliminated entirely. Transparency about costs related to group health plans is now a matter of law. The day has arrived when full disclosure of all compensation including contingent income received from carriers is now mandatory.

> *If you have any desire to make a significant impact in the healthcare marketplace, you need to be committed to driving change! You cannot afford to generate change while allowing someone else to determine the value of your leadership and professionalism.*

The transition to a fee-for-services model is a journey, not an event. Your next step is to commit yourself to the journey. Once you have firmly committed to this path, paint a picture in your mind of your ultimate destination. Start with the end in mind; then plot your course and set the wheels in motion.

We have provided this workbook to support your journey and provide a *Path* to help you embrace your transition from a commission-dependent employee benefits insurance agency to a thriving, profitable fee-for-services healthcare risk management consulting practice. As you launch on your journey, we are here to support you. Our plan is to offer interactive virtual workshops where we will provide deeper insight into the ideas and concepts presented in this workbook. If you are interested in participating in one of our workshops, please email us at workshop@thepath.biz.

Best wishes for a successful journey!

Endnotes

[1] "Historical," National Health Expenditure Data, CMS.gov, www.cms.gov/Research-Statistics-Data-and-Systems/Statistics-Trends-and-Reports/NationalHealthExpendData/NationalHealthAccountsHistorical.

[2] Craig Palosky and Sue Ducat, "Average Family Premiums Rose 4% to $21,342 in 2020, Benchmark KFF Employer Health Benefit Survey Finds," KFF, October 8, 2020, www.kff.org/health-costs/press-release/average-family-premiums-rose-4-to-21342-in-2020-benchmark-kff-employer-health-benefit-survey-finds.

Notes

Notes

Notes

Notes